D0171667

## Also available from the American Academy of Pediatrics

Caring for Your Baby and Young Child
Birth to Age 5*

Caring for Your School-Age Child
Ages 5 to 12

Caring for Your Teenager

Your Baby's First Year*

New Mother's Guide to Breastfeeding*

Guide to Toilet Training*

ADHD: A Complete and Authoritative Guide

Baby & Child Health
The Essential Guide From Birth to 11 Years

Heading Home With Your Newborn
From Birth to Reality

Waking Up Dry
A Guide to Help Children Overcome Bedwetting

Immunizations & Infectious Diseases:
An Informed Parent's Guide

A Parent's Guide to Childhood Obesity
A Road Map to Health

The Wonder Years

A Parent's Guide to Building Resilience in Children and Teens
Giving Your Child Roots and Wings

Less Stress, More Success
A New Approach to Guiding Your Teen Through College Admissions and Beyond

Sports Success Rx! Your Child's Prescription for the Best Experience
How to Maximize Potential and Minimize Pressure

For more information, visit www.aap.org/bookstore.

* This book is also available in Spanish.

# Food Fights

WINNING THE NUTRITIONAL CHALLENGES OF PARENTHOOD
ARMED WITH INSIGHT, HUMOR, AND A BOTTLE OF KETCHUP

Laura A. Jana, MD, FAAP
Jennifer Shu, MD, FAAP

American Academy of Pediatrics
DEDICATED TO THE HEALTH OF ALL CHILDREN™

**American Academy of Pediatrics Department of Marketing and Publications Staff**

Maureen DeRosa, MPA
*Director, Department of Marketing and Publications*

Mark Grimes
*Director, Division of Product Development*

Jeff Mahony
*Manager, Product Development*

Carolyn Kolbaba
*Manager, Consumer Publishing*

Sandi King, MS
*Director, Division of Publishing and Production Services*

Kate Larson
*Manager, Editorial Services*

Shannan Martin
*Print Production Specialist*

Peg Mulcahy
*Graphic Designer*

Jill Ferguson
*Director, Division of Marketing and Sales*

Kathleen Juhl
*Manager, Consumer Product Marketing and Sales*

Cover design by Stephen B. Starr Design, Inc.

Pencil drawings by John Regnier

Book design by Linda J. Diamond

Library of Congress Control Number: 2006930230
ISBN-13: 978-1-58110-244-4

The recommendations in this publication do not indicate an exclusive course of treatment or serve as a standard of medical care. Variations, taking into account individual circumstances, may be appropriate.

Statements and opinions expressed are those of the authors and not necessarily those of the American Academy of Pediatrics.

Products are mentioned for informational purposes only. Inclusion in this publication does not imply endorsement by the American Academy of Pediatrics.

CB0048

1 2 3 4 5 6 7 8 9 10

# WHAT PEOPLE ARE SAYING

*Food Fights* is smart, funny, and right on target. I recommend a big helping!
  *Harvey Karp, MD, FAAP*
  Author, book/DVD, *The Happiest Toddler on the Block*

*Food Fights* presents a no-fuss approach to helping young children develop the healthy eating habits that will see them through a lifetime. Its delightful tone makes it a joy to read, and refer to, over and over again.
  *Elizabeth M. Ward, MS, RD*
  Author, *The Complete Idiot's Guide to Feeding Your Baby and Toddler*

*Another fantastic* guide from Drs Jana and Shu! *Food Fights* helps parents find a realistic middle ground between what their child *should* be eating and what their child is actually willing to consume.
  *Lisa Singer Moran*
  Executive editor, *Baby Talk* magazine

*Food Fights* should be mandatory reading for anyone responsible for feeding an infant, toddler, or young child. In their characteristically easy-to-read, humorous fashion, these two pediatrician moms have created the perfect tool to help parents and caregivers instill healthy eating habits, avoid temper tantrums, dodge flying vegetables and, above all else, maintain a healthy attitude toward the nutritional challenges of parenthood!
  *Tanya Remer Altmann, MD, FAAP*
  Editor in chief, *The Wonder Years,* and editorial board advisor,
  *Healthy Children* magazine

*The authors* of *Food Fights* have done a great job! This book will go far in continuing to help parents lay the groundwork for excellent nutrition.
  *Sandra G. Hassink, MD, FAAP*
  Editor, *A Parent's Guide to Childhood Obesity: A Road Map to Health,*
  and director of the Weight-Management Program at the Alfred I. duPont
  Hospital for Children in Wilmington, DE

*E*ncouraging, *compassionate,* and clear for its compelling nutrition messages, this book will be a comprehensive source of information for any parent trying to guide their children to healthy eating habits and lives. I especially like how the up-to-date nutrition information is translated into real-life situations.

    *Connie Guttersen, RD, PhD*
    Author, *The Sonoma Diet*

*F*ood *Fights* gives thorough, practical, fun-to-read advice for parents as they tackle some of parenthood's most difficult challenges.

    *Claire McCarthy, MD, FAAP*
    Pediatrician, Children's Hospital of Boston; pediatrics instructor, Harvard Medical School; and contributing editor, *Parenting* magazine

*F*ood *Fights* makes it clear that raising children who are healthy eaters requires good role models for healthy eating. The tips provided throughout the book make it easy for parents to be those healthy role models.

    *Connie Diekman, M.Ed, RD, LD, FADA*
    Nutrition Consultant

*T*hank *you,* thank you, thank you Drs Laura and Jennifer—You did it again. Your new book, *Food Fights,* is a fantastic and much needed addition to my arsenal of informative and practical approaches to children's food idiosyncrasies. As a pediatrician in a busy practice, I know that the families in my care will both benefit and embrace your insightful ideas about helping children learn to make healthy choices. Your book is wonderful and is sure to help anyone who has ever struggled to make the climb up the food pyramid.

    *Emilio Arispe, MD, FAAP*
    Pediatrician, Methodist Physicians Clinic, Omaha, NE

*A*s *pediatricians* and moms, Drs Jana and Shu know that it's important to focus on good nutrition, but also to pick your battles. *Food Fights* offers reassuring and practical advice for parents who are worried about whether their kids are eating too much, not enough, or nothing green.

    *Diane Debrovner*
    Health and psychology editor, *Parents* magazine

*We have found that every family has at least one child who is particularly skilled at putting up a formidable food fight. With this in mind, we'd like to dedicate this book to our families' true champions, Sydney L. and Baby G.*

—LJ and JS

## ACKNOWLEDGMENTS

Writing the acknowledgment section of a book is actually much more challenging than one might think. After all—where do you draw the line? As working moms we couldn't have done it without the help of lots of people: last-minute babysitters, the in-laws who invited our children to come for a visit during our "crunch times," neighbors who helped keep our driveways shoveled, an operations consultant who helped keep Laura's school afloat, and good friends who didn't mistake our self-imposed disappearances as disinterest but rather as overcommitment. To all of them (and you know who you are): We would like to thank you for all of your encouragement and support. That said, we do want to recognize a few of the many fine individuals who helped shape this book.

It seems only appropriate that we start out by recognizing Laura's mentor, Dr Benjamin Spock. As one of the most influential figures of the 20th century, his insights and commitment to helping raise generations of healthy, happy children continue to serve as an inspiration to us both.

Even beyond the gratitude we have for the unwavering support of our families, friends, and colleagues, we also wanted to give special recognition to Laura's mother, Dr June Osborn. A pediatrician herself, she was convinced early on that this was a book that we needed to write and continually helped motivate us to finish writing it. And when it was—at long last—completed, she read it cover-to-cover to make sure that no "t" was left uncrossed, each "i" was dotted, and that every last split infinitive was reunited (except for the few we were too stylistically attached to to get rid of!).

We also owe special thanks to Dr Tanya Remer Altmann, a wonderful pediatrician and good friend who went above and beyond the collegial call of duty and pored thoughtfully over the many drafts of the manuscript.

As for keeping the true substance of *Food Fights* both practical and realistic, we have to extend our gratitude to all of the children we have had the pleasure of caring for, dining with, and/or the responsibility of feeding, all of whom knowingly (or unknowingly) served as test subjects for our book. A special thanks goes out to our own 4 children, all of whom are now of an age where they can actually read what we've written about them. They have certainly both humored and humbled us over the years. In addition, we appreciate all we've learned from the children we've cared for in our pediatric practices, not to mention those who attend Primrose School of Legacy—Laura's 200-student educational child care center, where the beauty of positive peer pressure is in full force at mealtime and the lunch menu has been known to include everything from cottage cheese, hummus, and spinach to ham-pickle-and-cream-cheese roll-ups.

Now that we have become better acquainted with the inner workings of the publishing world, and we've started actually reading what others write in *their* acknowledgment sections, we would be remiss if we didn't also acknowledge the supportive and hardworking staff in the American Academy of Pediatrics (AAP) Department of Marketing and Publications, including Maureen DeRosa, Mark Grimes, Jeff Mahony, Kathy Juhl, Kate Larson, Eileen Glasstetter, and Carolyn Kolbaba. We are well aware of how fortunate we are to be published by the AAP—an organization dedicated to the health of all children starting from the top with Executive Director Dr Errol Alden, to the more than 60,000 grassroots members who make up one of the largest children's health organizations in the world.

We can guarantee you this book would not be quite what it is today without the added insights and expertise lent us by our esteemed technical medical reviewers. They include

- Henry Bernstein, DO, dad and chief, Section of General Academic Pediatrics, Children's Hospital at Dartmouth
- Connie Diekman, MEd, RD, LD, mom and director of University Nutrition, Washington University in St Louis
- Sandra Hassink, MD, proud mom of 3, editor in chief of *A Parent's Guide to Childhood Obesity: A Road Map to Health* and director, Pediatric Weight Management Clinic, AI duPont Hospital for Children
- Melvin B. Heyman, MD, MPH, professor of pediatrics and chief, Division of Pediatric Gastroenterology, Hepatology, and Nutrition at University of California—San Francisco; chair, American Academy of Pediatrics Section on Gastroenterology, Hepatology, and Nutrition; and coauthor of *Feeding Your Child for Lifelong Health*
- Leann Lesperance, MD, PhD, mom and clinical assistant professor of pediatrics, SUNY-Upstate Medical University
- Claire McCarthy, MD, mom, author, pediatrician at Children's Hospital Boston, and contributing editor for *Parenting* magazine

- Scott Sicherer, MD, father of 5, associate professor of pediatrics and researcher at the Jaffe Food Allergy Institute at Mount Sinai in New York and author of *Understanding and Managing Your Child's Food Allergies* (Johns Hopkins Press 2006)
- Victor S. Sloan, MD, dad and rheumatologist
- Susanne Tanski, MD, MPH, mom and assistant professor of pediatrics, Dartmouth Medical School
- Elizabeth Ward, MS, RD, mom and author of *The Complete Idiot's Guide to Feeding Your Baby and Toddler*
- Claudia Zegans, MD, pediatrician and mother of 4

For reviewing the finer points as well as the fine print, we would like to thank parent-readers Zeynep Aksehirli, Katie Givens, Sarah Jeror, Julie Johnson, Leah Mosenthal, Koen Pauwels, and Teresita Weiss, Esq, as well as Dr Emilio Arispe, Denise Baddour, and Julia Cook for their ongoing support and encouragement.

And last but not least—when it came to the day-to-day reality of feeding our children (not to mention clothing, bathing, reading to, and chauffeuring them), we are most grateful to Alex and Ajoy—our selfless husbands who spent a disproportionate amount of their time *doing* it while we were preoccupied with *writing* about it!

TABLE OF CONTENTS

# introduction

CHAPTER 1

# food for thought

### Why Food Fights?

**We called this book** *Food Fights* for several reasons. First it was because we needed a catchy title to get your attention and, by the looks of it, we're off to a good start. The book is also called *Food Fights* because we hoped that the thought of a good old-fashioned food fight à la *Animal House* would be enough to make you smile, and the promise of a discussion of ketchup might be enough to make you both chuckle and breathe a knowing sigh of relief that we can relate to the *real* nutritional challenges of parenthood. But more fundamentally, it's because it is impossible to ignore the fact that food-related battles rank right at the top of the daily list of parental challenges, and they are being waged in virtually every household in America. Our children's nutritional fortitude is at risk and, as both pediatricians and parents, we decided it was high time to march to the front lines and mediate.

If you have ever asked yourself just how you are supposed to apply all of the latest dietary directives to your family's everyday life when your child recoils at the slightest hint of something green on her plate and you have a hard time even figuring out how to get dinner on the table in the first place, then this is definitely the book for you. If not, we can all but guarantee that you are still going to find plenty of tidbits of helpful advice that will serve you well. We are convinced that by giving you a bird's-eye view of what you're up against and arming you with some basic insights along with some palatable peacekeeping strategies, you can win the nutritional challenges of parenthood and play a defining role in shaping your child's lifelong eating habits. In order to do so, we felt it was important first to give you a big-picture perspective on the current state of affairs.

## Under Siege

As parents today we are faced with raising our children in a veritable minefield of dietary trappings and hazardous temptations. Finding them is not a matter of searching, but simply of opening our eyes to their presence in our children's everyday diets, not to mention our own. Over the past 2 decades, fast food meals increased from less than 10% to nearly a quarter of all meals consumed. Over this same time span, the percentage of total energy intake from either soda or juice increased nearly 100%, and salty snack intake doubled. Even bagels have been super-sized such that they contain at least 200 calories more than they did 20 years ago. Not surprisingly, the proportion of obese Americans has continued to increase as well.

Regardless of how you weigh the facts, it is impossible to look past the estimated 30% of adults older than 20 years (that's roughly 60 million people) who are now considered to be obese. At the same time, we know that children with obese parents are as much as 80% more likely to become obese themselves. These numbers confirm what we should have seen coming: An estimated 1 in 5 of our country's children have already followed in their parents' footsteps. Also hard to ignore are the clear health implications of poor nutrition, overweight, and obesity—including high blood pressure, diabetes, heart disease, eating disorders, and stroke, to name but a few. Despite ambitious goals for our country's collective weight reduction by the year 2010, things seem to be getting worse, not better.

So why tackle the huge problem of adult obesity in a book about teaching kids healthy eating habits? We hope the answer to this question is as obvious to you as it is to us: Because it's impossible to separate the two. While we had every intention of focusing our attention on the questions parents typically ask that are specific to their kids, we constantly found ourselves discussing eating habits in general. After all, if we as parents can't get our own eating habits and waistlines under control, how is it that we think we will be able to teach our children to do so? Bottom line: Our children stand to take after us in more ways than one, and when it comes to being overweight, they are already scrambling up the growth curves (at least for weight) in record numbers.

---

### 🍜 Weighing the Facts ☕

Since 1980 the Centers for Disease Control and Prevention reports that the number of overweight kids in America has more than tripled. Recent estimates suggest that 9 million children and teens between the ages of 6 and 19 are considered to be overweight.

---

So there you have it—a big-picture view of the battlefield. If that's all there was, it would be a very sobering sight indeed. Yet we are optimistic. If we weren't convinced there are things that each of us can do in our day-to-day approach to feeding our children that will help them steer clear of trouble and come out ahead, we wouldn't have bothered to write this book. Instead of throwing up our hands in surrender, we decided to take a closer look at what parents can do to prevent their children—and hopefully themselves—from becoming another statistic in this battle of increasing proportions.

### Looking Beyond the Substance at Hand

As much as this now seems like it's going to be yet another book on the subject of childhood nutrition, it's not. Well, not exactly anyway. While we fully intend to provide you with a reality-based approach to your children's nutritional needs and offer plenty of practical information for you to use as you whip up everything from your baby's first foods to your family's meals, this book is first and foremost about teaching, learning, behavior, and development. Because it really doesn't matter if you have a medical degree, a PhD in nutrition, or the best parental intentions in the world if you can't get your child to agree to the rules of engagement—get him to consider giving up his bedtime bottle, eat his peas, sit for a meal, or open his mouth and try new foods. Unlike so many of the nutrition books out there, this book is therefore as much about applying tried-and-true parenting skills as it is about the actual food. And while it may seem that in the end *Food Fights* is all about winning and losing, our real goal is to minimize food-related conflicts and take the fight out of food.

### Staying Away From Slippery Slopes

Part of the problem with parenthood is that nobody ever tells you just exactly on which day a nutritional necessity such as middle-of-the-night feedings or a bedtime bottle suddenly becomes a bad habit in the making. That's because as with most routines, using food for comfort and other such "food fights" ease themselves into existence while we're too busy going about our parenting business to notice. And while we don't presume to be able to give you an exact timetable of when to stop certain routines before they become ingrained, we intend to discuss many of the predictable slippery slopes of sustenance-turned-habit.

### Whetting Your Child's Appetite

We recently heard a comment that stuck with us like gum on a shoe: "It's one thing to place good food in front of your child, but it's altogether another to place the appetite for good food in your child's mind." We couldn't agree more. In fact, this astute observation serves as the underpinning for a good portion of what we aim to accomplish with *Food Fights*. While there are plenty of books that will promise you recipes for success and others that put lists of recommended vitamins and minerals at your fingertips, we hope instead to whet your appetite and empower you to establish an approach to teaching your children healthy eating patterns.

We strongly recommend you think of your role this way: You're planting the seeds of your child's future success. And as you may have already discovered, teaching children healthy habits doesn't happen overnight, and it's certainly not a one-shot deal. As with just about all tasks that involve nurturing children, you don't just go and plant seeds, take the time to water them, and then get frustrated the next day because there are no plants to show for your efforts. When it comes to modifying your child's behavior, be aware that it takes time and requires cultivation. Although we intend to help guide you down a path of nutritional (and behavioral) enlightenment, we guarantee that it will be a path with its requisite share of cookie crumbs and spilt milk.

## Setting the Table = Setting the Stage

It's next to impossible to discuss children's eating habits and nutritional status without taking into account several other factors. Not only do behavior and development play a key role in determining what your child is willing and/or able to accomplish at any given time, but your family's lifestyle stands to be a major influence. As we put together the advice we wanted to offer you in *Food Fights,* we kept wandering away from the table and confronting the entire "stage" of everyday life—everything from fast food to television, from work/life issues to hectic lifestyles.

Let's face it, being a parent today can be a bit tricky, and our goal is to point out how some of today's lifestyle challenges stand to impact your family's eating habits. We'll leave it to you to decide what, if anything, you want to change. And lest you start feeling pangs of guilt before you have even passed the introduction portion of the book, please realize that we do not mean to sit in judgment. Let us be the first to admit that our own schedules don't always allow for family-style meals, that keeping pace with the many demands of parenthood often means that our refrigerators sit empty, our kitchens go underused, and the waitstaff at some of the more family-friendly local restaurants know us by name.

**A Call to Action**

Despite the fact that we have high hopes for putting an end to many of the unnecessary food fights of everyday parenthood, let it be known that we do not believe in force-feeding you a rigid set of rules any more than we believe in force-feeding children. Instead, our call to action is to arm you with the information and inspiration you need to get started. By giving you realistic ways of putting nutritional guidelines into practice, our *Food Fights* plan of attack is designed specifically to help you keep your high chairs, family gatherings, and kitchen tables from turning into nutritional battlefields. We have yet to find a parent who wasn't grateful for a battle plan for winning the nutritional challenges of parenthood, and so we forged ahead and focused our efforts on creating just that.

CHAPTER 2

# war and peace

**It's one thing to acknowledge** that the childhood obesity epidemic is looming ever nearer and commit to protecting your child in this battle of epic proportions. It's altogether another to find the wherewithal at the end of a long day to appreciate your baby's unsuccessful but dedicated attempts to feed herself, leave the sippy cup at home, or stroll calmly down the aisles of the grocery store picking out produce you have the distinct feeling your child will never eat. Knowing what it is you're *supposed* to be doing, buying, and serving is a good step in the right direction. Knowing how to put your plan into action is a completely different story.

When we first sat down to address the most common dietary dilemmas that parents are faced with and write about how to successfully anticipate and win each of the most common childhood food fights, we found *ourselves* faced with an unanticipated struggle. We thought it would be easy to separate and address each unique challenge. Yet each time we tried to direct our attention to a particular food fight—whether it was bedtime bottles, soda pop, green vegetables, or ketchup—we found that today's wide-ranging battles aren't always as unique as you might think when it comes to handling them. In essence, we were recommending many of the same strategies over and over again, so instead of risking redundancy, we decided first to distill the common ingredients. What follows is the result: 10 overarching peacekeeping strategies designed to equip you with the skills you will need as your child's primary role model in matters of lifelong healthy eating.

## Palatable Peacekeeping Strategies

### Strategy #1: Vow Not to Fight Over Food

Half the parental "battle"—and we use the word intentionally because all too often the nutritional responsibilities of everyday parenting life deteriorate quickly into predictable battles—is figuring out how to teach your child healthy eating habits without ending up on opposing sides of the table. Right from the start, vow to yourself that you're not going to wage war over food—at least not so much that you find yourself worn out, frustrated, and/or feeling like a failure on a regular basis.

Despite the commonplace occurrence of food fights, the fact of the matter is that life's too short to pick many of these fights. If you get in the habit of truly fighting with your child over food, you're not likely to win in the long run. And more often than not, you're not likely to win in the short run, either. After all, there are few things harder than getting children to open wide when they don't want to, yet we've seen parents continue to try. One of the best things you can do is to commit to some basic ground rules on how you're going to approach matters of food, and then apply them as calmly and consistently as possible.

### Strategy #2: Remind Yourself That It's Not (Just) About the Bite

The other half of the battle is realizing that eating is not just about eating. It's about your parental expectations, the stages of your child's development, and more than a few habits—both good and bad—tossed in along the way. Just because we're talking about food doesn't mean that there aren't a whole host of other factors involved. You should remind yourself that feeding children is a learning experience for everyone involved, and parents and children alike are bound to bring far more to the table than just food or drink. Sure, understanding the substance at hand is fundamentally important, but it is also vital to grasp the opportunity we as parents have to teach our children healthy *attitudes* toward food and eating.

At the same time, it may be even more critical to recognize that eating is an activity that is particularly susceptible to a child's natural tendency to rebel. Your child's declarations of feeding independence stand to throw a wrench in your dietary plans and assert themselves in the form of food refusals, tantrums, and food-related rituals at just about the same time you nobly set out to introduce him to a wider range of foods and teach the social graces of eating.

As we have said before, mealtime is no exception to the rule that your child is going to test your limits. In fact, it's his job to do so, and rebellion and an occasional outright mealtime mutiny are only to be expected. Similarly, you have a lifetime's accumulation of your own individual, inherited, and even cultural beliefs regarding food, and we highly recommend separating out those factors that make each bite or sip a far more weighty issue in your own mind than it otherwise needs to be.

### Strategy #3: Never Let Them See You Sweat

We could just say, "Don't sweat it," but our years of experience tell us that unless you're far more calm, cool, and collected than we are as parents, you're going to sweat it out anyway. When it comes to feeding our children, everyone inevitably feels some degree of pressure to perform. So in the spirit of reality, instead of telling you not to sweat it, we suggest perfecting your ability to hide it when you do. We believe this is a practical strategy for parenting in general, but it will most definitely serve you well as you dish out what you know is best for your baby or child. This applies most often to those foods that children really want that they shouldn't have, or for things you really want them to eat but they want nothing to do with.

When it comes to babies, they may seem as if they aren't aware of how much of an emotional investment you may have riding on getting them to eat their rice cereal or drink out of a cup, but they nevertheless do sense stress and it can and often does wear off on them. The same holds true for toddlers and older children to an even greater degree. If they find out just how much their consumption of a single brussels sprout means to you, or how much of an impact a tantrum can have on pushing back their bedtime in favor of a late-night snack, they're sure to try it. When they repeatedly test your limits, your job is to stick to your guns and reinforce the ground rules while maintaining your composure.

### *Strategy #4: Keep Food for Food's Sake*

This important peacekeeping strategy seems, on its surface, relatively straightforward—just teach children to eat when they're hungry, drink when they're thirsty, and refrain from doing so when they're not and you've got it made. Sound simple? You'd think it would be since we are all born with a natural drive to eat and drink only as much as our bodies need. Yet the fact of the matter is that by the time we reach adulthood, and often far sooner than that, these internal cues are overshadowed by external ones, and too many of us eat and drink for reasons that have very little to do with hunger or thirst. It's pretty safe to say that the classic "freshman 15" pounds gained by those entering college isn't just the result of increasing hunger and the availability of better food, that enjoying a movie really shouldn't require a bucket of popcorn, and that a lot of football fans would be a fair bit slimmer if they didn't associate *Monday Night Football* with burgers, beer, and a bag of chips.

Whether you find yourself in the habit of offering your child food as comfort, convenience, or reward, realize that most, if not all, of these hard-to-break eating habits take root during early childhood. As soon as you start looking at it this way, you'll see everything from sippy cups to desserts in a new light.

### *Strategy #5: If at First You Don't Succeed…Try, Try Again*

This is perhaps one of the easiest strategies to say, but one of the hardest to actually stick to. After all, it's not exactly human nature to experience rejection and come back for more. Yet most of your child's eating and drinking skills are developmentally dependent. As we've said before, the improvement of your child's daily eating activities should be considered learning experiences. The ability to keep one's rice cereal in one's mouth and actually swallow it, use a spoon without dumping one's food, drink from a cup without spilling, and sit still at the table for any measurable amount of time all take time to master.

We would like to suggest that you approach the skills required for eating and drinking the same as you would when teaching your child her ABCs. You don't wait until the day before kindergarten before you sing the alphabet to your child. In fact, some parents start singing it to their babies even before they start to coo, and only with time, repetition, encouragement, and many "failed" renditions do kids respond; imitate; separate the *lmnop*; and eventually put *a* and *b* together in any sort of meaningful way.

The other aspect of maintaining a positive, can-do attitude in the face of rejection has to do with the actual food itself. Knowing that it can take a dozen or more exposures to a new food before a child decides to accept it will make it a little bit easier for you to swallow the reality of the preceding 11 refusals. The goal here: teaching tolerance. The measure of your success is neither how many tries it takes, nor the number of foods your child is ultimately willing to eat, but the instillation of a willingness to take a bite and try it.

### Strategy #6: Acknowledge Likes and Dislikes
Many a well-meaning parent has set out to teach food tolerance, only to be met with failure—even after employing every feeding strategy there is. The underlying and often overlooked problem: Just about nobody we know likes *everything*. We all have our distinct likes and dislikes, and children's attitudes toward food are no exception. We can also guarantee you that your children won't share all your likes and dislikes, that some tastes are more likely to be acquired over time (think blue cheese, grapefruit, and onions, to name a few), and some things are simply never meant to be. For Laura, it's cooked carrots. For Jennifer, it's raw ones.

### *Strategy #7: Eat by Example*

OK, so we've established the fact that everyone has their own likes and dislikes, and we've made the point that what starts in childhood stands a good chance of ending up an eating habit in adulthood. Now is as good a time as any to take a closer look at what *you* eat, when you eat it, where you eat it, and why. We're willing to bet that you have some habits that might not fare so well under nutritional scrutiny. You can decide for yourself not only if your pattern of eating is as healthy as you would like it to be, but also whether it is the example you want to set for your child because you can be sure he's watching you.

It is going to be a very hard sell to get your child to eat things that you yourself won't eat, or to make healthy choices when he sees you indulging your own frequent visions of sugar plums all throughout the year. And if you aren't in the position to change your own pattern of eating, we suggest you make a concerted effort to keep your less-than-desirable indulgences, habits, and dislikes to yourself. Once the jury has been biased (as is the case with beets and brussels sprouts in the Jana household), there's no good way to turn back.

### *Strategy #8: Opt for Out of Sight, Out of Mind*

No, out-of-sight tactics are not the most direct or enduring approach to teaching your child a sound eating style. But as a strategy for averting a battle, so long as your kids don't have money or a car at their disposal, restricted access works wonders and we highly recommend it. Kids of all ages are known to want what they see. At the same time, they are not very good at grasping the concept of delayed gratification, much less listening to reason if they can't have what they want.

If you don't want them to have it—whether it's a bedtime bottle or bubble gum—then don't set it where they can see it. You don't want your child begging for candy each night? Don't bring it into your home. You want to minimize the number of times you need to say no at the grocery store? Bypass the cookie aisle and choose your checkout lane wisely by avoiding the candy-laden ones. And by all means, minimize the amount

of time your child spends watching television, since most of the unbelievably large number of ads she'll be exposed to are for all those foods
and drinks she'd be better off not having.

### Strategy #9: Make Fun of Food

Food-related issues will undoubtedly be a consideration in every day of
your early parenting life. The topics, challenges, and approaches we've
chosen to discuss when it comes to selecting, introducing, preparing,
sharing, serving, and cleaning up foods are meant not only to help you
anticipate and effectively avoid some of the many potential food fights
that are known to lurk around every corner, but to help you actually
have fun in the process.

As you sit down to arm yourself with nutritional knowledge and
a strategic plan, we want to caution you against making food such serious business that you forget to enjoy the experience. Get your kids to
help grow a garden, have them help you cook a meal, even name the
end result after them (as in "Ryan's lasagna") and chances are good that
(a) you all will have a whole lot more fun doing it and (b) by getting
them to take ownership in the preparation, your kids will be more likely
to eat whatever it is you've collectively prepared. When all is said and
done, we hope you will have learned not to let the inevitable mealtime
mishaps get you down, that you'll be better able to savor the moments
both messy and neat and, in the end, that you will be empowered in
your efforts to restore not only peas but harmony to your family table.

### Strategy #10: Keep a Big-Picture Perspective

This strategy is meant to be applied to any and all food fights and help
you take the pressure off of both your child and yourself. The good news
is that there are no expiration dates on these strategies, and regardless of
whether your child is 5 weeks, 5 months, or 5 years old, it's still early and
you've got a lot of time to make an impact.

Simply think of your child's diet as a video rather than a snapshot,
and you're much more likely to end up with a clear picture of how you
can handle just about any food-related challenge that comes your way.

impact on your child's health, safety, and/or nutritional state of well-being. There should be little room for negotiation. These food fights are the ones most worth taking a stand on, even if it means holding your ground in the face of potentially fierce opposition. Fortunately, such pitched battles are usually few and far between.

- **3-Fork Food Fight: A Battle Is Brewing.** While 3-fork food fights are not to be taken too lightly and you'll still want to take heed, the stakes aren't quite as high and the end result of occasionally giving in or putting off the battle is likely to be of a lesser magnitude.

- **2-Fork Food Fight: Simply a Skirmish.** When you're on the battlefield, it's easy to make mountains out of molehills. Sure, you may have a point to make, and a very worthwhile one at that. But in the grand scheme of things, a 2-fork food fight is one you can put off until your child is in a good mood and you're not at the end of a long day. Or you can start looking to distract, entertain, or deter in ways that will defuse the situation altogether.

- **1-Fork Food Fight: Time for a Truce.** These are the battles that aren't worth fighting—the expected messes, behaviors, and challenges that are normal and to be expected. Instead of letting your feathers get ruffled, just pick up your fork and move on.

## Making Use of Mealtime Milestones

It's not hard to find charts that outline when you can expect your baby to roll, sit, and coo, or for your child to take his first steps, say his first words, and kick a ball. We thought it would be helpful if we compiled a list of similar milestones as they apply to drinking, eating, and all of the other factors that play into the many food fights we have chosen to address. You will therefore find milestones interjected throughout the book that will help you apply the well-defined developmental accomplishments of childhood to your mealtime routines—from when children can be reasonably expected to drink from straws or hold their own spoons to how long they should be capable of sitting still at the dinner table.

# PART II

# starting out on solid ground

CHAPTER 4

# baby bites: starting solid foods

### The Approach

As we begin our reality-meets-nutrition–based introduction to the world of "solid" baby foods and you venture to mix up your baby's first cereal and pop the top off your inaugural jar of baby food, let us set the tone by recommending that you treat the entire undertaking as a work in progress—for both you and your baby. As convenient as it would be to be bestowed with an infant who happily grabs a spoon—silver or otherwise—and devours a cup of rice cereal and pureed peaches before contentedly crawling away from the table clean as a whistle and happy as a clam, we have yet to see it happen. Rome wasn't built in a day, and neither is the ability to eat one's dinner daintily and independently in a white onesie. In order to introduce both solid food and fun into your daily routine, we suggest you pull up a high chair, grab a bib, get your camera, and make sure all of your rubber-tipped spoons are in a row because after months of eager anticipation, it's solid food feeding time!

### The Time for Food Has Come

Before the early 1900s, most babies were not fed solid foods until after their first birthday. By the 1950s, however, the feeding pendulum had swung far in the opposite direction, and infants were commonly given their first taste of baby cereal before they reached 2 weeks of age. As we continue into the 21st century, the current recommendation from the American Academy of Pediatrics is to wait until at least 4 to 6 months before introducing solids. Be careful not to miss your window of opportunity, however. Waiting much longer than 8 or 9 months to introduce babies to solids can make it more difficult to get them interested in giving up their full-liquid diets.

breast or bottle. For the first few weeks or more, you may find that
your baby can take it or leave it and, as a result, it is perfectly acceptable if some meals involve no solids at all.

- **Learn to Read the Signs.** What your baby thinks of each new food
  may be both smeared and written all over her face. Babies are known
  to have quite exaggerated responses to new tastes and textures, so
  don't be too surprised or too easily deterred if your introduction of
  a new food is met with a bit of spitting, scrunching of her face, and
  even a screech or two. If your baby proceeds to open her mouth for
  more, it's a safe bet that the rest (not to mention the mess) is just
  for show.

### First Servings: An Introduction to Baby Cereal

- **When Do I Start?** Once your baby is 4 to 6 months old and shows
  signs of solid-food readiness, you should be good to go.

- **Why Baby Cereal?** Infant cereals are relatively easy to digest and,
  more importantly, will serve as the primary source of iron in your
  baby's diet throughout the first year and potentially even beyond.

- **What Kind Do I Buy?** It's best to reach first for the single-grain
  cereals such as rice, oatmeal, or barley. They are considered to be
  the least allergenic and allow you to introduce your baby to one
  new food at a time (see Taking It One Day at a Time on page 200).

- **What Should I Mix It With?** You can use either formula or breast
  milk, although there's no harm in using water on occasion as well.
  You also have the option of buying jars of premixed infant cereal,
  although they technically offer no added benefit aside from convenience and tend to be fairly runny so you may find that you need
  to add some extra cereal once your baby gets used to the texture.
  After your cereal-feeding routine is well established, you can also
  feel free to add your baby's pureed fruits and/or vegetables into the
  mix instead of giving them separately.

**Solid Food Shortcuts—Cereal in a Bottle**

While the habit of adding cereal to an infant's bottle is one that has been around for a long time, there are several compelling reasons why you should not do so unless advised by your pediatrician (see "Refluxively Speaking" on page 221).

- **Ready or Not.** Your baby's digestive system is not going to be well prepared to process cereal until about 4 months of age. Once he's old enough to digest cereal, he should also be ready to eat it from a spoon.

- **Too Hard to Handle.** Offering cereal in a bottle (or even on a spoon) before babies are developmentally ready can bring with it an increased likelihood of gagging and/or inhaling the thickened mixture into their lungs. Unless there's a medical reason for giving it early, it's not worth jumping the gun.

- **Allergy Activation.** Early exposure to solid foods is thought to put babies at risk of developing food allergies in the future—a risk that can be minimized by simply waiting until the time is right (see "Allergies and Intolerances" on page 197).

- **Overfeeding.** Perhaps the biggest reason not to take the addition of cereal in a bottle too lightly relates to overfeeding. By instinct, your baby knows how much breast milk or formula to drink based on volume, not calories. While it is difficult to overfeed a baby when you're talking about breast milk or formula alone, as soon as cereal gets added in, things get a little murky—so murky, in fact, that putting cereal in the bottle is considered by some to be a form of force-feeding that can easily cause babies to "overdose" on calories.

- **How Should I Give It?** Definitely on a spoon, not in a bottle.

- **How Thick Do I Make It?** For the sake of clarity, we should point out that most babies' first servings of cereal fall far short of solid. Just how short depends on how well they take to textures, since there can be huge individual differences in just how much substance babies can handle. That said, the goal is to start out with a mixture that runs off the spoon, similar to the consistency of applesauce. If you happen to be a follow-the-recipe person, you'll be happy to know that every box of infant cereal we've ever seen comes with directions for mixing and dishing out your baby's first servings of cereal. Most

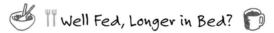

## Well Fed, Longer in Bed?

We sincerely wish it were true that a well-timed serving of rice cereal could transform previously poor sleepers into blissfully well-rested babies overnight. But the fact of the matter is that studies just do not support this commonly held belief. From a practical standpoint, it helps to distinguish between hunger and habit before betting on cereal as a sleep solution.

- **Cereal to the Rescue.** Some hearty eaters seem to become increasingly hungry and less satisfied with their all-liquid diets somewhere between the ages of 3 and 6 months. Despite already consuming upward of 32 ounces a day, they typically begin demanding more frequent feedings during the day and/or waking up to eat earlier in the mornings than has been their norm. If this pattern fits your baby, hunger may well be a culprit and you and your baby may, in fact, rest easier (and longer) as a result of adding cereal to his diet. Just be sure to touch base with your pediatrician first to discuss your options, remember factors other than hunger can cause a disruption in babies' sleep habits at this age, and that the 4- to 6-month recommendation for introducing solid foods into your baby's diet exists for good reason. Also, be forewarned that a significant improvement in sleep may not happen until your baby is eating at least a couple of solid meals a day.

- **Force of Habit.** If, on the other hand, your baby is perfectly content during the day but tends to wake regularly and want to eat frequently throughout the night, chances are good that force of habit is the cause of your sleepless nights rather than your baby's empty stomach. If your baby associates drinking with soothing himself to sleep, he is likely to end up demanding his "comfort food" every time he cycles through light sleep (see "Drinking and Dozing Don't Mix" on page 53) regardless of hunger or thirst. If this more accurately describes your situation, we're sorry to say that no amount of baby cereal is going to solve your sleep problems.

involve mixing approximately 1 tablespoon of cereal with 2 ounces of formula or breast milk. If your style is a little less calculating and a bit more go-with-the-flow (like ours, since neither of us ever bothered to measure), simply start by putting a spoonful or two of dry cereal into a bowl and then adding enough liquid to make the mixture thin and runny. Then let your baby be the judge. Too runny? Add more cereal. Too thick? Add more breast milk or formula.

- **How Much Do I Give?** Chances are your infant will let you know. If a few bites are all he wants, he'll probably turn his head and start fussing. If, on the other hand, his mouth is open like a baby bird and he squawks for more between every bite, it's a good bet you're not done yet. If you need a ballpark figure to aim for, eating any-where from 1 to 4 teaspoons at a sitting is a fairly standard starting point. Be prepared to mix up more, however, since this amount can increase considerably in a very short period—even over the course of several days.

### First Foods

Once your baby has a few weeks of cereal under her bib, she'll be ready for the wider world of baby foods. Whether you opt for the store-bought baby foods or choose to make your own, the questions often remain the same: figuring out how to correctly order your baby's foods (which

 At This Stage of the Game

Baby food manufacturers have made the first steps in baby food feeding more intuitive not only by selecting the foods and food textures that babies are most likely to handle, but also by labeling their jars by stages in an order you can follow as your baby's eating skills and interests progress.

- **Stage 1.** Stage 1 baby foods all share in common the fact that they consist of single ingredient baby foods—either fruits or vegetables. They often come in conveniently smaller jars for first feedings.

- **Stage 2.** Available in slightly larger containers, stage 2 baby foods also represent a step up in texture. In addition to being somewhat thicker, the contents of many stage 2 baby food jars contain a combination of ingredi-ents. This is also the stage where pureed meats first become available and are routinely added to the fruits and vegetables—often in the form of such baby favorites as apples and chicken or carrots and beef.

- **Stage 3.** As the jars become larger still, they are also more likely to contain additional spices and chunkier foods for babies on the verge of table food acceptance. Particularly texture-tolerant babies may be perfectly content to skip this stage altogether, favoring a quick jump from stage 2 baby food jars straight to table foods instead.

CHAPTER 5

# ⑂ it's not easy being green

**If only the Jolly Green Giant knew** the hostile feelings that were harbored against him, we're pretty sure he wouldn't be quite so jolly. And while we're on the subject, Kermit (with his beloved song, "It's Not Easy Being Green") could be a poster frog for one of the most classic food fights there is. We're referring to the resistance to eating green vegetables. It would be one thing if there were a distinctive taste shared by all green vegetables that could explain why, as a class of vegetables, they are so often rejected. But last time we checked, broccoli tasted nothing like spinach, nor could it be confused for green beans. And nobody can tell us that brussels sprouts don't have a smell, taste, and texture all their own. When it comes right down to it, nothing we can pinpoint links these vegetables together into a group that bears the brunt of table-time rejection. Nothing, that is, except for one unifying feature: They're all green.

## Not All Green Is Created Equal

Now before you resign yourself to the fact that the dislike of all green vegetables is inevitable, it is worth breaking down this issue into its component parts. What we're dealing with here are 2 simple things: the color green and vegetables. Suppose, for a minute, we adopt the theory that this is a green food revolt. That would make good sense if only all green foods were universally rejected…but they're not. Think Skittles and LifeSavers—and the argument falls apart. Even green apples don't suffer the slings and arrows, not to mention the humiliation, of being untouched, spit out, or thrown on the floor in the same way that green vegetables often do.

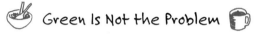

### Green Is Not the Problem

We're not buying the notion that green is to blame. Not when green M&Ms have been flying off the shelves since they were introduced in the 1940s as one of the original M&M colors, have since been singled out as aphrodisiacs and, on occasion, are sold in green-only packages.

This leads us to consider component #2: vegetables in general. We are well aware of the fact that some kids have issues with eating vegetables (see "Vegetables and the Great French Fry Conspiracy" on page 35), but why have the green ones been assigned the status of second-class citizens? We hate to point fingers, but given that this food fight can start long before peer pressure and anti-green propaganda can take hold, the only remaining logical answer is that it's our own darn fault. Somehow, somewhere along the way, we as parents intentionally or unintentionally bias our children against the very green vegetables we are so determined to serve them. We have put together the following strategies, along with a few observations, in the hopes of helping you teach tolerance and prevent this kind of judgmental behavior from becoming routine in your household.

### Sensing Your Disapproval

Consider for a moment whether or not *you* like green vegetables. If the answer is no, it makes it far more likely that (a) you don't follow the golden rule of eating by example, (b) your dislike will not go unnoticed, and (c) you don't serve them very often to your children. In a perfect world, simply making these observations would be enough to have you dishing out the peas and changing your own green-eating habits. But if this is wishful thinking and you prefer a more reality-based solution, then we suggest that you at least keep any and all asparagus-disparaging comments out of earshot of your children.

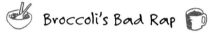

### Broccoli's Bad Rap

With a single discrediting remark made by an extremely high-profile parent, broccoli suddenly stole the limelight as the country's most notoriously disliked green vegetable. Shortly after being sworn in as the 41st president of the United States, and to the dismay of both parents and the broccoli growers of America alike, George H. W. Bush publicly declared, "No more broccoli on the White House menu." Shortly thereafter, truckloads of broccoli were deposited on the White House lawn in humorous protest. Who won the broccoli standoff? Broccoli's reputation was defended and as far as we can tell, ended up no worse for wear. And those who relied on the various food banks around the Washington area were the fortunate beneficiaries of a whole lot of broccoli!

### Good *and* Good for You?

You need only rely on a streak of perversity in human nature to predict that the more we're told something is good for us, the more we anticipate not liking it. Studies have actually shown that kids subscribe to and then act on the notion that whatever is supposed to be good for them can't possibly taste good. (Sort of like cod liver oil, which used to be routinely given to children by a generation of well-intentioned parents. When it came to actually swallowing this as a good thing, we're told it always left a bad taste in one's mouth.) Ultimately, the more time you spend discussing the relative merits of eating one's green vegetables, the more likely you are to trigger your child's disinterest, not to mention her "no" reflex (see "Food, Food Everywhere but Not a Bite They'll Eat" on page 87).

- **The Mashed Potato Fake-Out.** You don't have to be an Iron Chef to score big with your children by whipping up some pureed cauliflower as a mashed potato "fake-out." They'll be none the wiser if you just throw in a dash of salt and a smidge of butter and call them mashed potatoes.

- **Accessorize.** To your child, it may be all about the dip, but a celery stalk dipped in ranch dressing (or ketchup, for that matter) is celery nonetheless.

CHAPTER 7

# ꝩketchup for small fries

**We just couldn't write a book about** food fights without taking a somewhat lighthearted look at ketchup. Anyone who has played the role of a parent in the last century—or since 1872, to be more precise, when H.J. Heinz introduced his first version of modern-day ketchup—already understands why the king of all condiments warrants a chapter all its own. For some kids, just about everything tastes better with ketchup. Whether your family buys wholesale-sized bottles or makes sure that your car's glove compartment is always stocked with a few of the billion to-go packets of ketchup produced each year, you are not alone. The fact of the matter is that 97% of American households use ketchup, Heinz alone reportedly sells 650 million bottles a year, and not surprisingly, children younger than 13 eat 50% more ketchup than all other age groups combined. As parents, the condiment quandary we are thus faced with is this: Is keeping our children's foods ketchup-free a battle really worth fighting? More often than not, we have found that the answer is no.

### Mealtime Milestone: Taking Control

Two- and 3-year-olds need to feel that they are in control and want to do things on their own—a developmental milestone that can make for a messy mealtime and can also stand in the way of your attempts to scale down the volume of ketchup your child uses. Today's easy-to-squeeze, upside-down bottles only make it that much easier for kids to help themselves—unleashing their drive toward independence (and, along with it, significantly more ketchup). When kids take over the task of tipping, they have been found to use as much as 60% more ketchup than what they would be served by an accessorizing adult.

### You Say Tomato, I Say Condiment

Many children develop a definite tendency toward ketchup dependency. Starting in toddlerhood, dousing one's food with ketchup can become a daily dietary ritual. We're not exactly sure how ketchup's popularity came to be, but we have a couple of ideas. The first is simple popularity by association: French fries are the country's most consumed vegetable (see "Vegetables and the Great French Fry Conspiracy" on page 35) and ketchup almost always comes with the territory. We also have a hunch that it's because ketchup serves as compromise. Kids aren't exactly receptive to trying new foods or flavors, and ketchup serves as a palatable way to cover up the taste of just about anything. In either case, inquiring parents of ketchup-consuming kids are left to find the answers to the following questions:

1. **Do No Harm**—*Does allowing unrestricted ketchup use violate the parental responsibility to do no harm?* In other words—is the use of a lot of ketchup bad for your kids? While we certainly wouldn't go so far as to say ketchup is outright bad, it is probably worth pointing out that most ketchup does contain more than its fair share of corn syrup and/or sugar to help the nutrients go down, and 4 tablespoonfuls has

 Ketchup Goes to School

The question of whether or not ketchup could (or should) be counted as a vegetable took center stage in the early 1980s when the US Department of Agriculture proposed a novel approach to getting kids to eat their vegetables. They proposed that both ketchup and pickle relish would count as the vegetable portion of the 5 required school lunch food items (meat, milk, bread, and 2 servings of fruits or vegetables). We will stay out of the highly politicized debate over whether this was simply a way to reduce the cost of the school lunch program or a sincere attempt to offer a more palatable option and put an end to the fact that many a lima bean was going to waste. But we can tell you that the outcry was so swift and decisive against the "ketchup as vegetable" program that ketchup was not only taken off the vegetable list, but the powers that be quickly put a billion dollars back into the country's school lunch program.

a higher salt content than your average hot dog (which is quite a lot!). You may want to take that with a grain of salt, however, since ketchup is also packed full of the antioxidant lycopene and has proven itself time and again to be a very useful peacekeeping condiment.

2. **Drowning Out**—*Does allowing a child's palate to hide behind a protective barrier of ketchup have any long-term implications in her future acceptance of new foods and flavors?* Not that we know of.

3. **Earning Brownie Points**—*Does serving your child ketchup count toward good behavior?* First, does ketchup have any nutritional value? As nice as it would be to have all of the ketchup our kids consume count as healthy servings of vegetables, we're sorry to report that it would take roughly 4 tablespoons of ketchup to add up to the amount of nutrients found in a medium-sized ripe tomato. That said, if you're truly looking to introduce more vegetable servings into your child's diet, pound for pound or ounce for ounce, you're better off promoting tomato sauces or salsa (a rising superstar in the world of condiments, which usually consists of other vegetables as well as tomatoes). Practically speaking, however, there's no reason why the judicious use of ketchup shouldn't be part of a well-rounded diet—especially because it is so successful at increasing the likelihood that children will eat a much wider range of other healthy foods along with it.

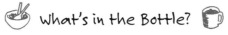

### What's in the Bottle?

Nutritionally speaking, ketchup typically contains strained tomato sauce, vinegar, sugar or corn syrup, onions, garlic, salt, and other spices. It stands alone as a condiment that contains all 5 of the basic tastes—salty, bitter, sweet, spicy, and "full."

### It Could Be Worse

If you find yourself with a child who would rather dine on ketchup sandwiches than eat anything you have to offer, and you cringe at the realization of just how much ketchup your household consumes, these

CHAPTER 8

# ⅋ the epic bottle

**In some families, giving the bottle** the old heave-ho is a mealtime milestone that comes and goes without much ceremony, struggle, or notice. For others, however, extracting the bottle from their child's daily drinking routine can be a very disruptive process, to say the least. The fact of the matter is that some kids (and parents) just don't want to let go, and parents are left searching for solutions.

So why should we (or you) worry about taking a stand and taking away the bottle sooner rather than later? After all, everyone ends up getting rid of their babies' bottles eventually, and to the best of our knowledge, no college application has ever asked, "At what age did you master the skill of cup-drinking and put away your bottle for good?" The reason for the rush is really quite straightforward: Because we are entirely convinced that this important drinking milestone doesn't get any easier the longer you wait. In fact, as time goes by and attachments grow stronger, it usually gets much, much harder to break the bonds that bind children to their bottles. Once toddlers' fierce independence gets involved, we have seen bottle-weaning battles last not just days or weeks, but months and even years. So instead of simply preparing you for a formidable fight, we want to give you a fighting chance of peacefully putting aside both the bottle *and* the battle.

### Why All the Put-Downs?

We acknowledge that it's only natural that children love their bottles. What's not to love? They represent just about everything that's good about being a baby: nourishment, bonding, calories, and comfort. But we have good reasons to suggest putting your child's bottle to rest as early as possible. On the way to toddlerhood, there develops a definite downside to drinking from the bottle: What starts out as an absolute nutritional necessity gradually becomes much less about the *need* to drink from a bottle and much more of a hard-to-break and unhealthy habit in the making.

 Bye-Bye, Bottles!

Both the American Academy of Pediatrics and the American Dental Association recommend that bottles should be bygones by the time children celebrate their first birthdays.

- **Going With the Flow.** It's quick, it's easy, and whatever is offered to toddlers in a bottle typically flows just a bit too freely for their own good. In fact, drinking from a bottle takes so little effort that babies and toddlers alike can literally do it in their sleep—a sucking skill that leaves much to be desired after babies reach a few months of age.

- **Drinking It All In.** Learning to taste a variety of foods and achieve a healthy balance in what they eat is especially important for toddlers during their formative feeding years. Yet because it's easier to suck than to chew, toddlers who still have ready access to their bottles often develop a distinct tendency to drink far more than they would otherwise, leaving them with little or no remaining appetite.

- **Sucking for the Sake of It.** Just because toddlers eagerly drink from a bottle does not mean that they are genuinely thirsty—even if they drink a lot whenever it is offered to them. Many babies and toddlers become reliant on sucking as a primary way of comforting them-selves—a well-recognized habit referred to as nonnutritive sucking. Especially when toddlers still want a bedtime bottle, or wake in the middle of the night demanding a bottle that quickly helps them fall back to sleep, chances are good that they are sucking for soothing's sake, not hunger or thirst.

- **It's What's on the Inside That Counts.** The problem with persistent bottle use lies not only with the bottle itself, but with what typically gets put in it. Even if milk and water are the *only* things that are ever poured into it, it can still turn into a problem of excess. But all too often, we also see toddlers being given additional, high-octane beverages—including juice, Kool-Aid, sports drinks, and soda pop. Once toddlers learn to associate the taste of this sort of "high" life with their bottles, you're guaranteed to have an even more difficult time taking the bottle (and these tantalizing beverages) away.

- **Cavity Considerations.** Clinging to one's bottle goes hand-in-hand with bathing one's teeth in sugary liquids. Subjecting a toddler's teeth to this sort of prolonged exposure to the elements is asking for nothing but trouble and invariably leads to cavities and tooth decay.

- **A Language Barrier.** It can be somewhat difficult to understand toddler talk to begin with. It makes it even harder when they spend a good part of the day with bottles stuck in their mouths. Like pacifiers, we believe there's a time and a place for bottles, but as soon as they get in the way of talking, we're all for setting them aside.

### Making the Connections: Bottles and Ear Infections

Studies suggest that the more time children spend lying on their backs while drinking from bottles or sucking on sippy cups, for that matter, the greater their risk of getting ear infections.

### Letting Go: The Bottle's Last Stand

For some parents, saying goodbye to the bottle is particularly difficult to do because it symbolizes saying goodbye to babyhood. For others, it's simply hard to figure out how to best go about it in the face of potentially fierce opposition. In either case, you'll want to have a good game plan in place.

> 🥄 **Mealtime Milestone: Solo Snoozing** ☕
>
> The fact that many babies actually need to be *taught* to fall asleep on their own may seem funny to some, but we guarantee you that it's no laughing matter. After all, falling asleep seems like one of those things that should just happen. Most healthy babies are fully capable of "hitting the snooze" without the aid of a parent, swing, car ride, breast, or bottle by the time they are 4 months old. While a few fortunate parents have infants who need very little instruction on the subject, rest assured that if your baby is drink-dependent, you are not alone.

### First Things First

When babies are first born, virtually all they do is eat and sleep. There is really not that much "awake" time to begin with, so it's often next to impossible to separate eating from sleeping. In fact, it frequently feels like eating and sleeping are one continuous process where eating results in sleeping, only to be interrupted by eating again. And in defense of all parents who have been led to believe that they are inadequate at preventing this pattern, we firmly believe that the newborn period *should* be all about eating and sleeping. In the beginning, not much time or effort needs to be directed toward trying to separate the two. That said, the day comes when parents go to sleep having been lulled into this typical newborn pattern, only to wake up and find themselves the not-so-rested parents of a 1-year-old who still requires a bottle at bedtime and insists on the need for midnight meals. Trying to divide drinking from dozing in the newborn period can be futile, but forgetting to do so in a timely manner is a setup for failure.

### Now I Lay Me Down to Sleep: Age-Based Strategies for Success

The following are simple steps you can take to help your child learn to separate drinking from dozing.

- **First 2 Months: Set the Stage.** In the first month or two, try to set the stage without expecting immediate results. Look for ways to make feeding time distinct from sleeping time—leave lights on, allow for

background noise, and keep your daytime feedings out of the bedroom as much as possible.

- **2 to 4 Months: Show Me the Way.** Between 2 and 4 months, start
  more actively attempting to separate mealtime from bedtime. Avoid
  the temptation to cram in one last feeding for good measure when
  your baby is clearly drowsy. If your baby does try to fall asleep
  during a feeding, see if you can rouse her either by playing, changing, bathing, or any of a number of interactive options designed to
  ensure that she won't grow accustomed to using a bottle or breast as
  her cue to fall asleep. Try also to resist the urge to feed your baby at
  times when you don't think she's truly hungry, and remind yourself
  that babies cry for reasons other than just hunger—including fatigue
  and overstimulation. And finally, make a concerted effort to lay your
  baby down before she is already asleep. Remind yourself that it's a
  very good thing for your baby to be left alone to coo to (and soothe)
  herself every now and then—especially at bedtime.

- **Older Infants: Handle the Habit.** After 4 to 6 months, the breast or
  the bottle may have already become your baby's signal for slumber,
  at least to a certain extent. As a direct result, drinking herself to sleep
  may become a requirement each time she wakes up during the night.
  At this point, we suggest shifting your focus to habit breaking. While
  habits can be tough to break, it is not too late to teach your baby
  bedtime independence—and along with it, to give everyone involved
  a chance to sleep on it.

### The 4 Bs of Bedtime

The reality of habits is that (a) they can be hard to break and (b) they
are not always bad. Take away one habit and you often need to find
something to take its place. In the case of the bedtime breast or bottle,
be reassured that we don't intend to leave you empty-handed once you
take away your baby's primary source of bedtime comfort. These 4 Bs of
bedtime will provide you with a soothing substitute that has proven to

be one of our most tried-and-true routines for bedtime success—both for babies and older children.

- **Bathing.** Baths are a soothing, hygienic, and decisive way of separating the evening's eating activities from sleeping. No way around it—only the unbelievably fatigued child will sleep his way through a bath. That means that when feeding time is over, your child will get the message that eating is not in any way, shape, or form a cue to go to sleep.

- **Brushing.** Whether you choose to do this right after the last feeding or just before the actual bedtime itself, we strongly encourage you to get in the habit of having a toothbrush (or washcloth or gauze—see "Brushing Up" on page 127) be the last thing in your baby's mouth at night (other than, perhaps, a clean pacifier during the first year as an added method of sudden infant death syndrome prevention).

- **Books.** We realize that we're supposed to be focusing our attention on food fights but want to share with you the fact that we've found nothing more suitable as a breast/bottle stand-in than books at bedtime. Bottom line: Since you don't want food or drink to become your child's bedtime source of comfort, books can serve as the perfect cue that it's time to cuddle up and go to sleep. Think about what happens when you're tired and you try to read? Bingo—you fall asleep. When it comes to lifelong healthy habits, we can't think of a better one.

- **Bedtime.** Short of drugging kids (which we don't condone, no matter how tired and tempted you might be), it's mighty hard to force a child to fall asleep. We suggest you stop trying and instead stick to implementing a routine time for your child to get ready for and get into bed. Once you've set the stage so that bathing, brushing, and books signal bedtime, you should just let your child fall asleep independently. Sure, this may involve some additional challenges, protests, and even the need to consult additional parenting resources (of which, we can assure you, there are many), but in the end we have always found that if you do a good job of making the bed, your child will learn to lie in it.

CHAPTER 10

# sippy cup syndrome

Sippy cups are like the training wheels of cup drinking. With leak-proof lids and spill-savvy valves, they effectively prevent messy spills along a child's path to independence and have earned their place as a mainstay of modern-day parenthood. So how, you might ask, did they earn a place in our book? Because sippy cups are so practical that they almost always have a way of overstaying their welcome. We find irony in the fact that parents spend considerable amounts of time trying to figure out how to get babies to drink from sippy cups, only to dedicate even more time and effort later trying to take them away. In our quest for convenience, not to mention spot-free carpets and cars, sippy cups often become a permanent fixture in our children's daily dietary routines. We want to address the question of just when the practical use of a sippy cup becomes problematic and provide you with some sippy cup tips and tricks of the parenting trade that will help you achieve the delicate balance between sippy cup success and outright overuse.

## Banishing the Bottle

The strategy of introducing a sippy cup early on is quite rational at the outset, since getting your baby accustomed to using a cup of any sort is a successful tactic to avoid bottle-weaning battles (see "The Epic Bottle" on page 47). The only real nutritional obstacle that stands in the way of getting rid of the bottle is when children haven't learned any other drinking skills to meet their daily needs. This can be overcome by planning ahead and making sure that your child has adequately mastered an alternative mode of drinking. Usually the solution is in the sippy cup. The good news is that most babies are developmentally ready to start learning to drink from a cup between 6 and 9 months—at an age well before stubbornness tends to set in. Within a couple of months, most become quite adept at sipping from a sippy cup.

### Mealtime Milestone: Drinking Directives

It's impossible to know when your baby is ready to rely solely on sippy cups, or to distinguish habit drinking from nutritional necessity, for that matter, without first taking into account what the daily drinking requirements are at different ages. When babies are younger than 1 year, they generally need no more than 32 ounces a day of either breast milk or formula, and contrary to popular opinion, babies technically need no water or juice. The drinking directive drops to about 16 ounces a day at the same time as the shift to cow's milk at a year.

## Drinking It All In

### Sippy Cup Tip #1: Go Valveless

The task of sucking on the spout of a sippy cup that has a valve in place generally requires significantly more sucking prowess than using a straw or a sippy cup without a valve, and you may find that it takes your child until her first birthday or later to master the sippy cup skill of drinking against resistance. By simply taking the valve out of the sippy cup lid and allowing the liquid to flow more freely, you are likely to lessen her frustration and increase her interest in drinking out of a cup. Just keep in mind that you're more likely to be in for some spills and plan accordingly.

### Lift and Separate

As a practical word of caution, be sure that when you lift the lid of your child's sippy cup for cleaning, you also take the time to separate it from its valve and wash both the valve and the spout thoroughly. Milk and any other liquids you may choose to serve all have a tendency to hide in nooks and crannies and turn into hidden moldy messes in no time. As you might imagine, this is not a pretty sight. Fortunately, every sippy cup we've ever come across has been dishwasher safe, and the dishwasher baskets designed to contain small baby feeding items are perfect for this purpose.

### Sippy Cup Tip #2: Start Cup Conditioning

When it comes to first sips, it's worth being aware that what you initially choose to put inside your child's sippy cup may count for more than you realize—both in how likely your child is to conform to this new custom and what she'll ultimately be willing to take away from it. Parents often choose to start off with water when first offering a sippy cup. That approach makes perfect sense from a mess-management standpoint, not to mention for future water acceptance and cavity prevention. However, the problem is that some children come to so firmly believe that anything *but* milk should come out of their sippy cups that they won't have it any other way—an expectation that can foil your breast- or bottle-weaning plans. We have found that if you first introduce your baby to the novel concept of a sippy cup by filling it with more familiar liquids (ie, formula or breast milk), you increase the likelihood that she'll be interested in embarking on this more mature manner of drinking, thus averting a future battle.

### *Sippy Cup Tip #3: Anticipate Sippy Cups Scorned*

Learn to go with the flow. If a traditional sippy cup just doesn't seem to cut it, you can always try a similar style of cup, but one that comes with a straw in place of a spout. While a straw cup may not be as effective in preventing spills, it can help you meet your child's nutritional goals, since many a sippy cup scorner does just fine with a straw. That said, there are a few holdouts who won't have anything to do with a sippy cup *or* a straw. If your baby happens to be one of them, don't lose sight of the fact that sippy cups are not a required rite of passage, and that this is likely to be a temporary problem at worst, and a blessing in disguise at best (see Sipping Down the Slippery Slope below). Feel free to set the sippy cup aside and try again later or skip it altogether.

### Sipping Down the Slippery Slope

We know very few parents who haven't owned one sippy cup (or 10). We both have carpets and cars that are unquestionably less the worse for wear because we spent years making full use of these simple and inexpensive solutions to spills. But after a healthy dose of hindsight, we have found ourselves compelled to issue a fairly firm parental warning: While sippy cups can understandably become a parent's best friend, they run the real risk of leading your child down a slippery slope of unhealthy habits.

Take a minute to think about how many of the toddlers you know—including your own—are in the habit of toting their sippy cups around with them as constant companions. As the objects of great affection, these practical pieces of plastic have somehow achieved a status that rivals security blankets, with evidence of their stronghold everywhere you turn—in cars, strollers, doctors' offices, child care centers, and even toy boxes all across America. This observation leads us to 2 very important nutritional questions: Do toddlers really need to drink that much and, either way, is this form of constant infusion good for them? The answer to both questions is no. Yet experience tells us that separating a toddler from his sippy cup is often far easier said than done. That's why we've decided to close out the discussion by sharing with you these final tips for sippy cup success.

### Sippy Cup Tip #4: Drink for Drinking's Sake

Set limits. Inherent in the use of sippy cups is that they enable children to drink when they might not otherwise be able or allowed. Limit sippy cup use to only those times when your child truly needs to drink. This involves not letting your child get in the habit of drinking while doing other daily activities, and especially not for the purpose of drinking and dozing (see "Drinking and Dozing Don't Mix" on page 53).

### Sippy Cup Tip #5: Avoid Roaming Charges

It has been said that the sippy cup is to today's toddlers what the cell phone is to teenagers. For both it is useful to set the rule (and stick to it) that no roaming is allowed. Try to restrict your child's sippy cup use such that most of the time, he drinks sitting down—ideally doing so along with a meal or snack. We can assure you that toddlers who are required to stop what they're doing and sit down at the kitchen table each time they want to drink are far less likely to slip into situations of overuse and dependency.

### Sippy Cup Tip #6: Keep It Short and Not Sweet

Toddlers love their sippy cups. And all too often they love the sugary liquids that fill them. Unfortunately, sucking on a sippy cup is not as unlike sucking on a bottle as you (or dentists across the country) might hope when it comes to inciting tooth trouble. Long after their bottle days are past, toddlers are still prone to the habit of bathing their teeth in the cavity-causing liquids commonly poured into their sippy cups and are at real risk of developing the same type of tooth decay. Our advice: Don't let your child slowly sip over long periods, since this is a surefire sign of habit drinking; and try for the most part to offer milk in a cup at mealtime and water between meals.

- **Cutting or Keeping the Fat?** Although all types of milk contain roughly the same amount of calcium, they differ considerably in both their fat and calorie content. Some parents have the tendency to oversimplify the role fat plays in their children's diets, assuming that less is best. While many adults could certainly benefit by reducing the amount of fat in their diets, a better understanding of fat's function in promoting early brain development has led to the recommendation that fat not be taken out of the diets of young children. For this reason, experts now agree that children should not be switched from whole to reduced-fat milk before they reach 2 years of age. After that, however, the need for higher-fat milk has been seriously questioned.

 Fat Facts

For the sake of comparison, the amounts of fat and calories contained in each 8-ounce cup of the various types of milk are listed below.

| | | | |
|---|---|---|---|
| Whole milk | 4% fat | 8 grams fat | 150 calories |
| 2% milk | 2% fat | 4.5 grams fat | 120 calories |
| 1% milk (low-fat) | 1% fat | 2.5 grams fat | 100 calories |
| Skim (nonfat) | 0% fat | 0 grams fat | 80 calories |

## Milk Milestones

The following is an age-based approach to figuring out just what kind of milk you should be pouring for your child and when.

- **Younger Than 1 Year: No Milk.** At least not regular cow's milk, that is. Younger than a year, the only types of milk children should be given are breast milk and/or formula, and generally no more than 32 ounces a day at their peak (around 6 months). If babies are drinking any more than that, more food may be in order.

- **1 to 2 Years: A *Whole*-some Approach.** Children younger than 2 years need more fat than older children and adults to keep up with their rapid growth and brain development. That's why roughly half of a toddler's daily calories should come from fat, and why whole milk has proven itself to be such a useful source. At the same time that your child makes the switch to cow's milk, however, the amount he should drink drops to a total of only two 8-ounce cups a day.

- **2+ Years: From Thick to Skim.** After age 2 years, we are all better off limiting our fat intake to no more than a third of our daily calories. Switching your child to low-fat or preferably nonfat (skim) milk is one of the quickest and easiest ways to help your child make this cut. Two cups of either is recommended for children 2 to 8 years and 3 cups for everyone 9 years and older.

### Getting Rid of Unnecessary Milk Fat

Some kids hardly notice the difference when you switch what they are drinking from full fat milk to low-fat or nonfat. Others grow so accustomed to the creamy richness of whole milk that they have trouble acquiring the taste for anything less. If you find that your child needs to be eased into the healthier habit of drinking skim milk, simply try reducing the fat content more gradually: Start by swapping out whole milk for 2% and then wait a while before reaching for the 1% and eventually the skim.

---

### Buttering Them Down

When cooking packaged foods such as macaroni and cheese, Hamburger Helper, or Lipton Pasta Sides, you can decrease the amount of unnecessary fat by using skim milk or extra water when the recipe calls for milk and by omitting the butter completely.

---

### The Changing Roles of Milk

#### Too Much: Milking It for All It's Worth

When it comes to milk, it is entirely possible for children to get too much of a good thing. Every now and then, we come across toddlers who drink milk for all it's worth, and then some. This is most typically true of children who are allowed to continue drinking out of their bottles well past their first birthdays, and/or those who make use of sippy cups to drink milk before, during, and after meals. Not only does overconsumption of milk leave children with little or no appetite for food, but it can cause some serious constipation and even lead to iron deficiency and anemia.

If you find your child has trouble drinking her milk in moderation, try any or all of the following to lower the volume to a more reasonable level:

1. **Give It in a Cup.** Drinking out of a bottle makes it way too easy for kids to consume large amounts with very little effort. Pouring the milk into a cup instead will definitely help reduce her intake (and jump-start the bottle-weaning process).

2. **Make It Milk With Meals.** Instead of letting your child sip on milk throughout the day, you can put in place more appropriate limits by only serving milk with meals and then offering water with snacks.

3. **Give Food First.** If milk is taking the place of meals in your child's diet, give her food first, *then* milk. Be prepared to stand firm, offer water instead of milk as needed, and be aware that this necessary step may lead to an initial tantrum or two.

### Too Little: When Kids Just Say No!

In a different twist to the milk challenge, you may find that your once milk-loving child wakes up one day and wants nothing to do with it at all. This scenario tends to happen for one of several reasons, all of which require patience and a commitment to try, try, try again.

- **A Change in Delivery.** One of the earliest and most common causes for self-imposed milk abstinence has nothing to do with a dislike of milk itself, but rather what it is served in. When children are switched from a bottle to a cup, even those who *love* their milk may stubbornly refuse any and all offers. Unless babies are introduced at an early age to the notion that water (and juice, if you must) is not the only thing that comes out of a cup and that milk can legitimately come out of something other than a bottle or breast, they can all too easily become conditioned to believe that milk has absolutely no business being in their cups. If you're already months past the option of making the introduction early, you may be in for a battle before your child is willing to drink milk again. While we do recommend that you keep offering it in a cup (and avoiding the temptation to return to the bottle), you can buy yourself some extra time by serving your child alternative calcium-containing foods (see page 71) or asking your pediatrician about calcium and/or vitamin D supplements.

- **As a Matter of Taste.** Some 1-year-olds are simply slow to warm up to the taste of cow's milk, and it can take weeks or months instead of days for them to adjust. If this describes your situation, try blending your child's more readily accepted breast milk or formula with a gradually increasing amount of whole milk until your baby gets used to the different flavor and consistency. For example, start by mixing three quarters of a cup of breast milk or formula with a quarter cup of whole milk for a few days, then go to half and half, and then continue to increase the proportion of cow's milk at a pace your baby will tolerate.

---

### Some Like It Hot

If your child has always had the luxury of drinking warm breast milk or formula, he may start out with a chilly attitude toward drinking his cow's milk cold. In order to encourage him to warm up to the idea of a nice cold cup of milk, you can feel free to heat it up just enough to take the chill off and get him to drink it. Then gradually serve it cooler and cooler and it shouldn't be long before he's perfectly happy with it coming straight from the refrigerator.

---

- **Food Takes Over.** From the day your baby is introduced to solid foods, you will be in charge of managing the balancing act that involves keeping her from favoring food over drink or vice versa.

Regardless of what kind of milk you're pouring, it is always a good idea to keep an eye on your child's overall consumption. If it drops below the level where it should be, consider whether food has taken its place and is filling her up. If so, simply offer milk *before* the meal instead of during or after, and give it with snacks if necessary.

- **Drowned Out.** For children of all ages, the biggest ongoing challenge that milk inevitably comes up against is falling into disfavor. Plain and simple, milk can be (and often is) drowned out by other drinks such as juice and soda pop—both of which offer very little in return. Even water—which is good for kids if not overdone—sometimes gets in the way of milk consumption.

### Sweetening the Pot

In a perfect world, all children would drink their milk straight up—no added sugar, no added color. But the fact of the matter is that many don't—making the option of sweetening it to get them to drink it all the more tempting. While the last thing most kids need is more added sugar, in the grand scheme of things, flavoring milk with a bit of chocolate or strawberry powder is a relatively minor trade-off to keep up their calcium intake. Just remember not to jump to this option too quickly or continue it for too long if it's not absolutely necessary, since it can easily become a dependency.

### In Search of Substitutes

Despite your best efforts, some children just won't drink milk. If your child isn't getting his daily amount of calcium from milk—whether it's for the short-term or the long haul—there are fortunately many substitute sources that can provide you with peace of mind while providing him with this important mineral. The major downside is that unlike milk, few products also contain vitamin D, which helps the body absorb calcium, so you may need to aim higher when using these alternatives.

## Calcium in Comparison

| Alternative Sources | Serving Size | Milligrams of Calcium |
|---|---|---|
| Soy milk, calcium-fortified | 1 cup | 300 |
| Yogurt | 1 cup | 300–415 |
| Orange juice, calcium-fortified | 1 cup | 300 |
| Cheddar cheese | 1½ oz | 300 |
| Pizza, cheese | 1 slice | 220 |
| Macaroni and cheese | ½ cup | 180 |
| Ice cream | ½ cup | 88 |
| Waffle, enriched | 4-inch | 77 |
| Orange | 1 medium | 50 |
| Cereal, ready-to-eat | 1 oz | 48 |
| Sweet potatoes, mashed | ½ cup | 44 |
| Chewable calcium supplements | 1 tablet/chew | 100-500+ |

### And Finally...Too Late

By the time kids reach 1 year of age—and sometimes many months sooner—milk given at bedtime generally serves no purpose except to cause trouble. Not only is it almost certain to be well beyond the nutritional call of duty, but it is also likely to be given in a bottle, damage teeth and, despite popular perception, disturb sleep. That's why we strongly suggest serving the last drink for the day at dinnertime. If you're not convinced, we suggest flipping to "Drinking and Dozing Don't Mix" on page 53 and/or "The Epic Bottle" on page 47.

CHAPTER 12

# water works

### What About Water?

What we find most notable about water is its striking absence in the daily drinking routines of many kids. Given the fact that most parents we know start out eager to give their babies water to drink, and most babies we know are more than happy to oblige by sucking, sipping, or even lapping away, we found ourselves wondering how it is that water finds itself so consistently wiped off the kids menu in a matter of a few short years. After brief consideration, we've decided it all boils down to the fact that water gets drowned out by juice, soda pop, and any of a whole host of more tantalizing yet nutritionally problematic beverages that make their way into our kids' cups, sippy cups, and even bottles. We therefore figured it was well worth putting together a quick refresher course on how to instill your child with a healthy attitude toward water and help her maintain a taste for this nearly tasteless drink.

### First Fluids

After spending many months on a singular diet of breast milk and/or formula, you might think that babies would react to the idea of mixing things up a bit and drinking anything new with disinterest, distrust, or even outright disdain. But more often than not, babies seem to take to water like fish do, and your earliest challenge with water will not be how to get your baby to drink it, but in judging just how much you should be giving. The following are a couple of standardly accepted guidelines for good measure.

- **Younger Than 6 Months.** Although many parents find it hard to believe, babies actually need no water at all until they're at least 6 months old. That's right: We said you need not add water (except of course for the water used in any formula preparation). That is because babies get all the fluid they need from breast milk and/or formula. In fact, giving young infants more than an occasional sip or two of water may fill them up enough that they drink less of their calorie-rich alternatives.

- **Older Than 6 Months.** While this is as good a time as any to introduce water into your baby's drinking routine, realize that he still probably doesn't actually *need* much. After babies reach 6 months of age, it is generally agreed upon that you can give 4 to 6 ounces of water a day if you so desire. Remember that once solid foods enter the scene, your baby will also be getting a fair bit of water from the solid foods he eats as well as from what he drinks.

 Not So Solid Solids

If you are interested in keeping track of just how much water your child gets on any given day, don't forget that water comes in many shapes and sizes. In addition to the water content in the liquids she drinks, be sure to factor in any of the many water-logged foods that may make up your child's diet on a day-to-day basis—all of which provide some water. The following are examples from the American Dietetic Association of fruits, vegetables, and other foods that all contain a relatively high percentage of water.

| | |
|---|---|
| Lettuce | 95% |
| *Water*melon | 92% |
| Broccoli | 91% |
| Carrots | 87% |
| Yogurt | 85% |
| Apples | 84% |

## Going With the Flow

By the time your child reaches toddlerhood and as long as he's getting enough milk during the course of the day, we suggest offering milk with meals and water with snacks. This not only ensures that drinking water becomes a regular habit, but also leaves less room for juice and/or soda pop to take over (see "A Revealing Look at Pop Culture" on page 79).

## Is Wetter Better?

Once you've got a toddler who happily drinks water, the next step is to ask whether you should consider water to be a case of the more the merrier. While some water is good, more water is not necessarily better. There are several instances in which water can pose a problem.

- Some kids embrace their water-filled cups and bottles with open arms, so much so that they let water fill them up. While filling your belly with water may be a commonly recommended dieting tip for adults trying to quench their appetites, be sure not to let your child fall short on her caloric intake.

- The younger or smaller the child (especially infants younger than 6 months), the more at risk she is for something called *water intoxication*—a serious condition where drinking excessive amounts of water causes sodium levels in the body to drop to a potentially dangerous level.

- Be aware that every now and then, a child's love of water and/or excessive thirst can be a sign of an underlying medical condition. Don't hesitate to contact your doctor if your child starts to show a sudden major increase in drinking water.

## 8-a-Day?

The only frame of reference most parents have when it comes to just how much water we should all aspire to is that "they" say we should make a habit of drinking eight 8-ounce glasses of water a day. Who are "they"? Just about everyone we know. Of course that doesn't mean that they're all doing it—just that this "8 × 8" dictum is universally touted as the right thing to do in the name of good health and happy kidneys. That said, you might be interested to know that a Dartmouth College kidney specialist decided several years ago to try to find out whether this was based on scientific fiction or fact. Just where did "they" get their information? The best he could come up with was that somewhere along the way, the Food and Nutrition Board of the National Research Council recommended getting approximately "1 milliliter of water for each calorie of food"—a recommendation that translates into approximately 2 liters (about 64 ounces) of water a day! Unfortunately, the sentence that followed this recommendation and which stated that most of this quantity could come from foods seems to have gone unnoticed as the water-guzzling obsession ensued. Either way, 8 × 8 ounces a day was never intended for children.

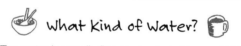 What Kind of Water?

- **Tap water:** Tap water is usually fine to give to babies and kids alike. In the United States, it is not necessary to boil tap water before giving it to healthy children. If you have reason to be concerned about the quality or purity of your water, you can consult your pediatrician, check out the annual report from your water supplier, or call your local health department.

- **Bottled water:** Bottled water has become quite trendy, and is admittedly a convenient albeit more expensive option. Just be aware that most bottled water lacks fluoride (see page 77), is not necessarily any cleaner or safer than drinking tap water, and the flavored versions, although colorless, can hide unnecessary sugar or artificial sweeteners.

- **Well water:** If you plan to give your child well water, you'd be well advised to have it tested first. The high nitrate levels sometimes found in well water can interfere with oxygen delivery in the blood and cause a potentially serious illness in young infants called *methemoglobinemia* or *blue baby syndrome*. In addition, other contaminants may be present.

### Don't Forget the Fluoride

Ever since fluoride was added to the public water supply in the 1940s, there has been a dramatic decrease in tooth decay. Because fluoridated tap water is often taken for granted as a local public health measure, its benefits are sometimes overlooked in the areas of our country that do not have it. Add to that the fact that so many people drink only bottled water these days, and chances are that a lot of kids are going without this useful mineral. The Centers for Disease Control and Prevention recommends that kids from 6 months to 16 years get fluoride, either in their drinking water or as a supplement. Before 6 months, fluoride supplementation is not recommended, and parents concerned with overexposing their babies to fluoride—which has the potential to cause changes in the tooth enamel—should check with their local water utilities to see how much is in their water supply. Another option: to use low-fluoride bottled water (usually labeled as "purified," "deionized," "demineralized," or "distilled"). By talking to your pediatrician and/or dentist, you can make sure your child is getting the proper amount of fluoride. Also be sure to read "Brushing Up" on page 127 for plenty more tooth-saving tips.

### Last Call

The way we see it, giving kids a drink of water before bedtime has become a common but often unnecessary practice. While we endorse the idea of giving kids a glass of water if it's in the place of milk or other bedtime beverages, doing so really isn't routinely necessary and usually doesn't add up to anything more than a habit or a delay tactic. Most kids can make it through the night without needing to drink by the time they are a year or so old. In addition, drinking at bedtime ups the odds that your child is going to have to pee during the night. That's why we suggest doing away with the last drink of the day altogether, at least until it becomes crystal clear that it's not becoming a dependency and that having a cup of water at your child's bedside isn't going to be cause for trouble.

CHAPTER 13

# a revealing look at pop culture

**You Say No Soda, I Say No Pop**

Having worked together for years but grown up in 2 different parts of the country, we only recently discovered that we call soft drinks by 2 different names. Jennifer says soda, Laura says pop. But one thing we can agree upon when it comes to soda pop and our kids is that we both want to call the whole thing off. The real food fight challenge here is first to convince yourself that it is a battle worth fighting, and then to muster the resolve to keep your child away from the lure of soda pop—a noble cause that is admittedly much easier said than done. Whether you're talking orange, brown, purple, or colorless—one thing seems crystal clear: Once kids develop a fondness for the flavor of soft drinks, there may be no turning back. Before you wave a white flag in surrender to the industry, however, we'd like to arm you with some facts to help you take the fizz out of the soda pop fight.

The Soft Drink Sensation That Has Swept the Nation

We are, after all, referring to a $65 billion a year industry. Soft drinks have found their way into our hearts and homes (and schools, no less!). The resulting challenge: The American Academy of Pediatrics now estimates that somewhere between 56% and 85% of kids drink soft drinks on a daily basis.

### So What About Soda?

Let's face it, soda pop tastes good. Really good. So good, in fact, that an overwhelming number of parents we know can't even resist the urge themselves. And experience tells us that if you are as likely as not to find yourself with can in hand, you may casually decide one day that offering your offspring a sip every now and then couldn't do any real harm. Let's face it, a sip here and taste there is usually how the "addiction" starts—whether on special occasions such as at a birthday party, in a restaurant, on an airplane, or in the comfort of your own home. Do the math, however, and all these sips can add up to a lot of sugar, not to mention a strong likelihood that your child will acquire an unquenchable thirst for more. So before you proceed with a single-sip strategy, we suggest you take heed: One sip may be more than enough to turn your toddler into a popaholic and have you flipping frantically to our "Whining and Dining" chapter on page 95.

### Sobering Sugar Statistics

It is very hard to ignore sugar as a major culprit as we take a closer look at the unhealthy eating habits of our children and the war being waged on obesity. Contemporary kids get more than twice the recommended daily amount of sugar, most of it from soda pop and other sweetened beverages. Once you are aware of the fact that each 12-ounce can of soda pop contains the equivalent of 10 teaspoons (almost ¼ cup) of sugar, it becomes easy to see how having just one soft drink a day can increase a child's risk for obesity by 60% and even harder to look past the fact that soda pop really is nothing short of liquid candy. Enough said, except to remind you that most sodas have been super-sized in recent years so that bottles or fountain drinks may contain 20 ounces or more instead of the previous 12.

### 🍜 A Juice Box ☕

Parents who try to justify juice as a healthier option may be surprised to know that a 12-ounce serving of 100% grape juice contains 1½ times as many calories as grape soda, and that a recent study found 100% fruit juice to be no better than soda pop. The fact of the matter is that sugar is sugar when it comes to teeth, calories, and drinking problems. If and when you choose to give your child juice, you can use the following guidelines:

- Make sure it's pure fruit juice—since fruit drinks that aren't 100% juice typically contain sweeteners such as high fructose corn syrup that up both the cavity and calorie antes.
- Hold off on introducing your child to juice for at least his first year and refrain from serving it in a bottle.
- Limit the amount he gets to no more than 6 ounces a day.
- Dilute your child's juice with water.
- Whenever possible, serve juice that contains pulp for added fiber.
- Buy only pasteurized products (shelf-stable juices, frozen concentrates, or specially marked refrigerated juices) to avoid potential diarrhea-causing infections.

### Soda Pop Special Effects

#### Bothersome Bubbly

You don't need us to tell you that the carbonation in soda pop can cause gaseous emissions. It's already hard enough to get kids who have newly discovered the ability to burp on demand to cease and desist. Consider whether you want to add fuel to the fire by filling your child up with not-so-hot air.

#### The Caffeine Kick

We assume that most of you have firsthand experience with the effects of caffeine so instead of belaboring the point, just consider this question: Do you really want to be responsible for a child that gets revved up when she drinks it and grouchy when she doesn't? It is generally accepted by most health and nutrition experts that caffeine is not good for kids. And as a matter of convenience, caffeine can pose a real challenge to even the best-trained bladders, not to mention those that are still in training. In practical terms, this means more peed-in pants and party dresses!

### A Poor Place Kicker

Soda pop can fill up your child's stomach and leave little room for much else—whether that means taking the place of milk or simply serving to decrease your child's overall appetite for much healthier fare.

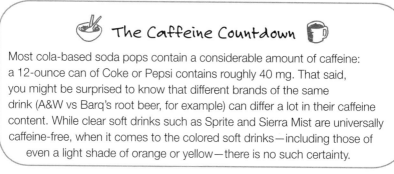

## The Caffeine Countdown

Most cola-based soda pops contain a considerable amount of caffeine: a 12-ounce can of Coke or Pepsi contains roughly 40 mg. That said, you might be surprised to know that different brands of the same drink (A&W vs Barq's root beer, for example) can differ a lot in their caffeine content. While clear soft drinks such as Sprite and Sierra Mist are universally caffeine-free, when it comes to the colored soft drinks—including those of even a light shade of orange or yellow—there is no such certainty.

### Strategies for Success

1. **Put Down the Pop...**or at least try to take your own sips discreetly. Your child is far more likely to do as you do than as you say, and this is a perfect opportunity for you to be a healthy role model. Limit your own soda pop intake—at least when you are in the presence of your child if not altogether.

2. **Mark It Absent.** There is a nationwide goal to get soft drinks out of our public schools by the year 2010—a noble goal that is more likely to be met the more parents commit to becoming actively involved in their children's schools. In the meantime, we certainly hope you don't wait that long to keep it out of your home, since stopping the pop at home is the healthiest choice and one you have far more control over.

3. **Limit the Load.** If you choose to give your child soda pop, try to hold off as long as possible and keep it within moderation. What is considered "within moderation"? While there's really no agreed-upon amount, we personally suggest giving no more than the equivalent of one can a week at most. Just remember: the less, the better.

4. **Consider It Dessert.** Soda pop (or juice for that matter) should be counted as a dessert. That way, children grow up realizing that soda, juice, cake, ice cream, and all other sweets are something to be enjoyed as once-in-a-while treats—not something to take the place of a real meal or more nutritious drinks.

# PART IV

# activities of daily eating

CHAPTER 14

# food, food everywhere but not a bite they'll eat

**It is often said that a parent's job** is to place a variety of healthy foods in front of their children, and it is a child's job to follow through and eat it. We absolutely agree. It's just that what sounds great in theory doesn't always play out in real life. More than any other food-related complaint, we have found that it's hardest for parents to cope with kids who just won't eat. Many parents can't help but worry that their children aren't getting enough vegetables, fruit, milk, or even food in general. So when push comes to shove, it can prove to be exceedingly difficult to keep from pushing *and* shoving food in front of our children in the name of getting them to eat what we're convinced they need. While your parental goal is to make sure that your child ultimately reaches something resembling nutritional harmony, the good news is that achieving it can take far less in the way of food or intervention than you might think.

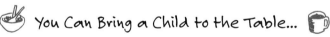 You Can Bring a Child to the Table...

… but it's very unrealistic to think you can force him to eat. Remember that you're not just trying to get dinner into your child's mouth but trying to put healthy lifelong eating habits into his head. Although it may not always seem like it, children are born knowing when they're hungry, and they quickly learn to do something about it. Conversely, they also know when they're not. If parents aren't thoughtful in their approach to ensuring that their children don't starve, they run the real risk of messing up these well-tuned internal controls.

## Why Kids Don't Eat

Since the problem of food refusal seems to be so prevalent, it's worth addressing why it is that so many kids refuse to bite. The way we see it, there are several potential reasons worth reviewing.

1. *A Matter of Misperception:* They actually are eating enough, you just don't realize it.

2. *A Matter of Appetite:* They're simply not hungry.

3. *A Matter of Principle:* They may well be hungry, but either their pickiness, their budding independence, or their need for control gets the best of them.

4. *A Matter of Illness:* Kids may refuse to eat before, during, and even for a week or so after they are sick (see "Feeding Through Sick and Slim" on page 189).

## Enough Is Enough

When contemplating whether or not your child is actually eating enough, one of the first things to consider is if, by any chance, you have exaggerated expectations. In other words, what do you consider to be enough? This involves asking yourself a few simple questions: Does your child really not eat one *single bite?* Or is it that she doesn't manage to polish off everything on her plate? Is she falling off her growth curves (see "Keeping Up With the Curves" on page 175), or just eating and growing like a normal kid?

### Watchful Weighting

One of the best ways to determine that your child is getting enough to eat, despite what it may seem like at the table, is to keep tabs on how his growth curve is shaping up. While the very few bites he takes here and there may have you convinced he's going to wither away, consistent weight gain and a well-rounded growth curve can provide you with reassuring evidence to the contrary. If, on the other hand, your child's weight is *not* keeping pace, then the advice in this chapter is not meant for you and you're best off enlisting the help of your pediatrician (see "Keeping Up With the Curves" on page 175).

### ⑂ The Clean Plate Club

For some parents, "not eating a bite" actually means that there's still some food left on the plate at the end of the meal. Today's parents (and grandparents) constitute generations of adults who likely spent their childhoods being told that the meal wasn't over until one's plate was licked clean. For those of you who were subjected to this nutritional philosophy-turned-food-fight, you'll certainly recall that the argument often continued something like this: "…and there are starving children in China, India, or Africa who would be very grateful for what you've left uneaten on your plate." Aside from the fact that it always led us to wonder just how one might actually get one's leftovers sent overseas, this method of mealtime management sends the wrong message by emphasizing quantity over quality (with some guilt added in for not-so-good measure).

Unfortunately, recent studies suggest that more than half of Americans have now earned their membership in what we call the Clean Plate Club by adhering to the policy of eating everything that is put on their plate—often leading to significant overeating. We strongly suggest that you break this cycle by focusing less on how clean your child's plate is at the end of any given meal and more on what you serve her in the first place. We are convinced that this quality-over-quantity approach to feeding will serve you well, and help your child grow up with a healthier attitude toward food that includes knowing when to say enough is enough.

### Appetite Lost

There are several factors that can easily account for a child's lost appetite, some of which may surprise you.

- **Food.** That's right, food! If your child's missing appetite seems most apparent at mealtime, snacking may well be the cause. Parents often forget to factor in what they—or other well-intentioned caregivers, friends, and relatives—have given their children to nibble (or feast) on throughout the day. Yet it doesn't take much for between-meal treats to add up to a considerable amount of food and calories. Some kids snack a lot—in some instances equal in amount, if not in substance, to a full meal or two. For others who aren't such big eaters to begin with, even a few late-afternoon cookies or crackers are enough to ruin their chances of being hungry for dinner. In either case, instituting limits on snacking such as no-snacks-allowed-within-an-hour-of-mealtime can help improve meal consumption.

- **Drink.** Kids who drink a lot also tend to run out of room for food for the simple reason that milk, juice, soda pop, and water can all be quite filling. Prolonged use of bottles and/or sippy cups can make it much easier for children to "drink their dinners." If your child is drinking too much, tracking down the source and slowing the flow is a reliable way of recovering a lost appetite.

- **Sick of It.** Children often lose their taste for food as much as a day or two before any other signs of being sick show up, and even a stuffed-up nose can easily get in the way of both eating and drinking. After their fevers, coughs, and runny noses are gone, children's appetites still may not return for a week or more (see "Feeding Through Sick and Slim" on page 189). Given that children come down with as many as 10 colds a year, you're sure to find that the common cold will occasionally factor into your child's disinterest.

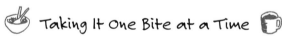

### Taking It One Bite at a Time

As you set your sights on achieving balance in your family's diet, we suggest you take the pressure off of your day-to-day efforts. After spending the first year or so of your child's life keeping very close track of how much goes in and out, it's important to realize that as your child gets older, you can allow for a lot more daily variation. After all, think about your own eating habits. Don't you have days when you're less hungry than others? Days when you just don't feel like eating something you usually like? Well, the same holds true for kids. Instead of meal-by-meal or day-by-day, set weekly goals and you'll find your approach to be easier, more realistic, and therefore more successful.

### Mind Over Hunger

The tendency for children to exert their independence starts in toddler-hood and persists through, well, forever, as best as we can tell. In fact, we consider striving for autonomy to be one of a child's most important lifelong tasks. Rising to the challenge of walking and rolling, figuring out how to dress and undress, and learning to feed themselves are all developmental milestones of independence that we generally look forward to. But along with these much anticipated achievements comes one of the more challenging aspects of a toddler's commitment to take control: the stubborn food refusals that drive most parents crazy. If there's one thing we can tell you to save you unnecessary stress, it's to expect your toddler to be finicky about food. Because when a toddler's will gets in the way, it's best to work with it, not against it.

### Think Big but Start Small

Be forewarned that dishing out a heaping helping of just about any-thing your toddler isn't familiar with can result in super-sized sabotage. Not only are you more likely to think your child hasn't eaten "any-thing"—since a few spoonfuls can easily go unnoticed in a monstrous mound—but your toddler is likely to perceive the plentiful portion as far more intimidating than a more realistically sized single serving. It's OK to think big, but take our advice when serving anything new and start out small.

### Mealtime Milestone: Suitable Serving Sizes

Portion distortion is the phrase fittingly used in recent years to describe the trend toward larger serving sizes. To avoid falling into this trap of over-serving your child, limit your first servings to approximately 1 tablespoon per year of age. If your child is two, 2 tablespoons of whatever you're serving should suffice. If he wants more, he will definitely let you know!

## ¶¶ Getting to Yes!

Starting at around the age of 2, nearly all children reflexively answer just about every question with the word "No!" and are quick to reject new things—especially new foods. Even the most adventurous of children may be utterly unwilling to add anything fresh to the menu. Attempting to force them to eat at this stage of the game is a battle you're doomed to lose. That does not, however, mean you need to completely surrender. Enter "no thank you" bites.

### No Thank You Bites

First—what is a no thank you bite? It is nothing more than a single bite of anything your child has predetermined that she doesn't like. If and when you are faced with mealtime protests, calmly sit back and tell your child you don't expect her to eat all of whatever you have served her. Instead, assure her that she has the right to say "No (more), thank you" after eating only one bite. Not half of what is on her plate, not 5 bites, just *1 bite* and then you will drop the subject. Not much to ask for, really. Usually the hardest part for parents is to remember to follow through on this strategic plan. Once you've committed to it, don't go back on your end of the bargain by expecting anything more.

   Now some of you might be wondering what this accomplishes. A lot, actually. Not only does the option of a no thank you bite take considerable pressure off your child to eat and create a more enjoyable, low-key mealtime experience, but it also gives her back a certain amount of control in the process. Best of all, you are likely to find your child actually asking for no thank you bites in the future. This may represent one small bite for your toddler, but it's one giant step toward making the most of her "no" reflex *and* increasing the odds that routinely rejected foods will be given a fighting chance of future approval.

### The 10th Time's the Charm

Believe it or not, studies suggest that it can take 10 to 15 exposures to a new food before a child accepts, much less likes, it. Without knowing this fact, if you're like most parents, you are likely to (a) default to serving only those foods you know your child will eat or (b) take the optimistic route and try serving new foods, only to quickly cross them off your future shopping lists as soon as they're met with initial disapproval. By simply continuing to offer your child foods regardless of the early rejection they may receive, you are likely to find that the second, third…or 10th time's the charm!

## Holding Out

You want to know one of the most common reasons why kids refuse to eat what's served to them even if they're famished? Because children are smart, they know what they want, and they are quick to learn how to get it. If you waver in your conviction about what you've placed in front of them *or* about your long-term nutritional goals, they'll soon discover that if they hold out long enough, they'll be served something "better." We hate to say it, but it really isn't so different from a game of chicken that kids are sure to win if they realize that their parents will always give in first. It happens all the time—especially to parents who become so concerned that their children aren't eating that they will settle for anything over nothing. If you find yourself in this situation, don't be afraid to call your child's bluff; tell your child and yourself it's OK for him to skip an occasional meal in protest of something he doesn't like. Just be sure to have his original dinner or something relatively healthy (and not some sugary treat) waiting for him in the wings the next time mealtime rolls around.

Also avoid the temptation to default to short-order cooking and offering your child alternative fare every time he balks at what you've served him. If you start out with and stick to a what-you-see-is-what-you-get approach to meals, your child will learn it's not worth his time to test your limits or make unreasonable mealtime demands.

CHAPTER 15

# ¶¶ whining and dining

**According to the dictionary,** whining is defined as complaining through the use of a high-pitched or distressed cry. By our definition, whining is an incredibly annoying yet seemingly unavoidable part of childhood that at the end of a long day can have the same effect as fingernails on a chalkboard. Children are quick to learn that whining can be an extremely effective way to get what they want to eat everywhere from the crib to the kitchen table to the grocery store. It's not hard to see how a child's persistent whining about food can cause a parent's nutritional decision-making abilities to become temporarily impaired. After all, it is a whole lot easier to yield to whining for food rather than something you just can't give in to—bubble gum flavored medicine or gummi bear vitamins, for example.

Knowing how terribly tempting it can be to give in to whining and dining for the sake of peace and quiet, we decided to offer you a quick review of the developmental building blocks needed for children to make use of more mature (and less irritating) negotiation skills, address what we have found to be the 4 most common reasons why children whine about food, and then help you more clearly see how to steer your way toward a future of finer dining.

### Mealtime Milestones: What's in a Whine?

- **9 Months.** Starting as early as 9 months, kids learn to point at what they want, including food.

- **12 Months.** Children typically utter their first words, and "no" is often one of the stand-alone favorites.

- **2 Years.** By this age, you can expect your child to put 2 words together— as in "no way" or "want that."

- **2 to 3 Years.** Kids begin to make better use of basic manners such as "Please" and "Thank you." This, in turn, allows for the development of the characteristic "puhleeeeeeeze" so commonly employed in the context of whining and dining.

- **3 Years.** At this age, kids can typically string together 3 or more words in a single sentence, and 90% of what they say is supposed to be understandable to the innocent bystander. This means that the "I want one!" or "I don't like it!" is likely to come through loud and clear for all to hear.

- **4 Years.** A more sophisticated form of whining may ensue, including the classics: "How come she gets to have one and I don't?" "You never give me anything good!" and "Please, just this once can't I...."

## Why Whine?

1. **Kids want what they can't have.**

   Whining for forbidden food is extremely common before, during, and after mealtime. In other words, anytime. And studies show that the more you forbid certain foods altogether, the more your child is going to want them.

2. **Parents want kids to eat something the kids don't want.**

   You say broccoli, they say no way...or they spare the small talk and simply whine, complain, and ultimately refuse to bite. While we enthusiastically support the idea of exposing children to new foods (see "Food, Food Everywhere, but Not a Bite They'll Eat" on page 87), we want to suggest that if you resist the temptation to force them to eat everything you serve, the amount of protest whining is sure to subside considerably.

3. **They are tired.**

   Children in general come equipped with less-than-perfect coping skills, and whining can show up unexpectedly at any time of day. That said, it tends to rear its ugly head more often when kids are tired and cranky. Now just think about when your child is most likely to be tired: lunch before naptime, dinner before bedtime. Need we say more? Given the timing of when we typically try to feed our kids, whining about food may not be about food at all, but rather about the circumstance—mealtimes simply end up in the crossfire of fatigue and crabbiness, with whining as the predictable result.

4. **Just because…**

   We have resigned ourselves to the notion that the onset of whining is as inevitable as rolling over, learning to walk, and puberty. It just happens. Granted, kids *are* more prone to whining when they're exhausted or hungry and are even more likely to employ this mode of dining dissention if and when they've tasted success with past whining efforts, but most of us will be faced with whining regardless.

### Whining Away

When you find yourself faced with a child who whines about food, the best thing you can do is come to the table prepared.

- **Expect the Expected.** Simply being aware that whining about food (and just about everything else) is inevitable will hopefully allow you to prepare yourself and keep it from grating on your nerves quite as much as it otherwise might.

- **Keep Your Cool.** Whining is an intuitive way for your child to get what she wants. It's also her way of luring you into battle. We highly recommend that you refuse to take part. If it's food she wants, then resist the urge to give it to her when the whining intensifies and you find you can't take it anymore. If whining is met with reward—or even if you hold out but it becomes clear that it drives you nuts— you can expect the agony to be prolonged.

- **Let Whining Fall on Deaf Ears.** Once your child is old enough to really get into the swing of whining—usually around 3 or so—start reinforcing the fact that her whining is going to fall on deaf ears. If she is sitting at the table whining about what she does or doesn't want to eat for dinner, tell her as calmly as you possibly can that you can't understand her when she talks like that and ask her if she has something to tell or ask you. If she continues to whine, go about your business. If, on the other hand, she makes an attempt to rephrase her "request," be sure to acknowledge her efforts. Remember that stopping mid-whine is a tough task at any age, so don't expect her to drop the whine entirely. It's not settling for less to respond to a toned-down snivel.

CHAPTER 16

# cutting corners

### Quirky Is in the Eye of the Beholder

If you stop to think about it, quirky eating habits really aren't bothersome at all…unless they happen to be somebody else's. Most adults we know, ourselves included, have certain eating habits that defy explanation—many of which, we might add, started in childhood. One or the other of us has been known to methodically cut corners off food, have a distinct preference for food not to be touching, opt for a drink straight from the can rather than from a cup, and harbor a dislike of hot food served on plastic. We find that it is exactly these types of little customs and routines that can prove quite perplexing, if not downright annoying, to others who have to live with them.

### When Children Beg to Differ

Coping with (and justifying) one's own quirky habits is one thing. It is altogether another when one's children start to become picky about their food if for no other reason than because they are inherently unable to keep their preferences to themselves. And picky they do become almost without exception, whether it's their food's shape, size, color, texture, or temperature. When day after day your child insists on having the crust taken off his bread, his orange juice strained, or his food lined up in straight little rows, you may begin to suspect your child is trying to irk you or drive you crazy—especially if you happen to be the type of parent who couldn't care less if your corn crosses the line and commingles with the meatloaf on your plate. Unusual food-eating behavior and food preferences or "rules" that start in early childhood usually boil down to this: For some often-unapparent reason, children decide that they don't like a food unless it's presented to them in a certain way. With no basis in science or nutrition, we suggest that you concede the fact that food rules usually defy reason and are going to be logical only to those who subscribe to them. That said, it is our goal to help you swallow what may be required of you as the parent of a picky eater, while helping you to know when to say when.

### Catering to Quirks

If your child develops what you consider to be peculiar eating habits, you will need to decide just how much you should (and can) tolerate. Avoid wasting time wondering "Why should it matter?" since the answer is simple: "Because it does!"…to your child, anyway. Bottom line: If a particular presentation or eating routine is within reason and helps with your child's overall food acceptance, it is often worth accommodating. Since "within reason" means different things to different people, we have come up with the following questions for you to ask yourself when deciding just how much you should cater to your child's quirks.

- **Can They Go It Alone?** Consider whether or not your child can satisfy her own quirky "needs." While peeling, slicing, and dicing can take a while to master, and handing over the Ginsu knife to a 2-year-old would be outright negligent, you certainly don't need to spend the next 10 years removing crusts yourself.

- **Is It Nutritionally Problematic?** If the only things your child will willingly put in her mouth are candy and Coke, you've got a problem on your hands. If, however, your child's unusual habits are a question of appearance or presentation, chances are good that she is not going to be in nutritional danger any time soon. Even in instances where children are picky about colors (see "It's Not Easy Being Green" on page 31) or entire categories of foods (see "Vegetables and the Great French Fry Conspiracy" on page 35), if you continue to offer a wide variety of foods, you will probably have some nutritional room to spare before you need to start worrying.

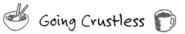

## Going Crustless

We decided to take a look at why it is that so many kids tear the crust off their bread, and better yet—why so many parents seem to care. We found not a crumb of evidence to suggest that the crust is in any way nutritionally superior to the rest of the loaf, or that this is a genetically determined trait. At the same time, chances are good that many of you pulled off a few crusts in your day as well, yet still scold your children for following suit (now that it's a quirk you no longer claim as your own). Why the contradiction? We can figure out no logical reason for this common parenting protest except for pure habit. In the spirit of reconciliation, we therefore want to assure you that it's not a big deal for crusts to be left behind. If you happen to be a parent who struggles with tolerating crust removal, you may be interested to know that more than one company has taken it upon itself to come up with a solution to this age-old food fight. Products such as Uncrustables and IronKids Crustless bread have "cut out both the work and the crusts for you" and are now readily available on grocery store shelves.

- **Is It Socially Unacceptable?** Although we're sure they exist, we actually have a hard time thinking of examples where a habit seriously crosses into the realm of social unacceptability. As long as your child doesn't insist on eating under the table or sticking her fingers in other people's food, the most you're likely to be faced with is having her refuse a meal at someone else's house if it's not prepared to her specifications. Just remember to adjust what you consider to be acceptable behavior as your child gets older, since what you can expect from a toddler is going to be quite a bit different than what you'd wish for from a 10-year-old.

- **Does Anyone Stand to Get Hurt?** Quirky eating habits are not usually cause for injury. Unless your toddler becomes set on eating only small, round, hard objects that match the size of his airway (see "All Choking Aside" on page 229), it's unlikely that anyone will end up any worse for wear.

- **Is It a Sign of Something More?** In some instances, dependency on very set routines, quirky habits, and repetitive behaviors can all signify underlying anxiety- or stress-related disorders. If you wonder whether your child's tendencies fall outside the realm of normal, give your pediatrician a call.

- 🍴 **Can You Take It?** Especially for those parents with very few of their own eccentricities to account for and/or very little time on their hands, coping with a picky eater can be likened to listening to the sound of grinding teeth. Some of us are more sensitive than others, and there's only so much one can take. This is really what picky eating and food fights come down to most of the time. All reason aside, it's OK to halt the habit if your child has some quirks you just can't tolerate no matter how hard you try.

## No Matter How You Slice It,....

Laura's grandfather used to insist that no matter how you slice or serve food, it's all destined to end up in the same place. This he said as he routinely ignored all boundaries and piled his (and everyone else's) plate high in what separationists could legitimately refer to as a food free-for-all. Clearly he didn't care nearly as much as many kids (and some adults) do about keeping food separate on the plate. The way we see it, respecting your child's food-related boundaries will serve you well because Laura's grand-father's philosophy has one major fundamental flaw: All food ends up in the same place—but only if it makes it past your child's mouth!

CHAPTER 17

# ꗠꗠꗠ food as a reward

**Everyone knows that candy makes kids happy,** and just about every
parent we know (ourselves included) has used this to their advantage by
bribing their children with sweets at one time or another. Even doctors,
dentists, bankers, and hairstylists have figured out that the promise of
a lollipop works wonders on a child's demeanor and his ability to hold
still, open wide, use good manners, or sit quietly. It's tempting, we know,
because using food as a reward works.

It only stands to reason that the temptation to do so is strongest for
those behaviors in which parents have the most vested interests or feel
the most pressure to perfect or eliminate—either for the sake of public
approval or for their own sanity. We have found that getting children to
eat falls squarely into these categories of behaviors. After all, doling out
a few M&Ms here and a cookie there doesn't seem like too high a price
to pay to bring out the best in your child's social behavior (eating or
otherwise). But try as we might, we can find no way around the fact that
the use of less-than-nutritious "prizes" has inherent contradictions when
it comes to winning the nutritional challenges of parenthood. If you
are able to avoid using food as a reward, then we applaud you whole-
heartedly. For most of you, though, we want to be sure you have a clear
understanding of what's at stake so that if and when you do choose to
use this popular method of behavior modification, you are fully aware of
just what it is you are getting yourself into.

In general, offering children sweet treats does achieve the desired behavioral results—at least in the short-term. Why? Perhaps it is because babies are born with a preprogrammed preference for sweet tastes over all others (salty, bitter, or sour)—a preference thought to have served them well over the ages. In days of old, and even now in developing countries, infants who took well to the sweet taste of breast milk were more likely to survive. For most of us, however, a sweet tooth rarely has anything to do with survival, but the penchant clearly remains.

### Table-Time Tradeoffs: In the Name of Healthy Eating

As ironic as it may sound when you stop to think about it, perhaps the most common way in which parents use food as a reward is to encourage children to eat more and/or "better" foods. You hear it all the time—the old "if you eat your _____ (you fill in the blank), then you can have _____ (again, you fill in the blank)" technique. While your child may eat what you want her to and end up with dessert to show for it, in the long run you are likely to end up getting your just desserts as well. We recognize that this tried-and-true technique may seem to work well at first, and we're well aware of the fact that practically everyone does it. But we suggest you proceed with caution because it runs the serious risk of backfiring for several fundamental reasons.

- **Things Can Quickly Go From Bad to Worse.** From a child's perspective, if you have to bribe them to eat something, then it can't possibly be good. If a child is indifferent to squash, making a big deal out of her eating it and bribing her to do so is, in fact, likely to foster a much more active dislike. Studies show that bribing children to eat certain foods causes them to resist eating those foods even more than if they had just been left alone.

- **The Tables Can Be Turned.** Part of never letting your children see you sweat (see Strategy #3 on page 11 of "War and Peace") is not letting them know just how much parental self-worth you have riding on each morsel. Let's face it—at its core, offering children edible incentives is really a way of manipulating them to do what you want. If, however, your child becomes aware of just how invested you are in what she eats—and children are very good at figuring this out—then look out! Kids who are "paid" to eat can become quite skilled at learning to turn it around to their advantage and either eat or refuse to do so as a way to get what *they* want. Once your child catches on, you may well be the one left with pie on your face.

---

### 🥢 Buyers Beware: Candy as a ☕ Quick Fix

We feel there should be a "Buyers Beware" warning in any and all candy-containing checkout lanes at the grocery store: If you use this candy as a quick remedy for unacceptable shopping behavior, you are sure to pay a much higher price than what you will be charged at the register. By offering candy in exchange for good behavior, your child will quickly learn to do what should reasonably be expected of him only in return for treats.

---

- **Elevating the Status of Forbidden Foods.** When you promise your child a scoop of ice cream in return for taking a bite of her dinner, what you perceive as your accomplishment stands to be quite different from what your child takes away from the meal and the deal. Instead of developing a newfound appreciation for the healthy foods you've managed to get her to eat, they become nothing more than a means to an end. Your child's sole focus is going to be on the sweets she's earned in return. In fact, you'll probably end up elevating the status of whatever goody you've offered as a bonus—making it more desirable than ever.

- **Learning to Follow Your Lead.** If your child isn't hungry but really wants whatever tantalizing food lies at the end of the meal, she may wind up eating more than she would otherwise. In this instance, all you stand to teach her is to ignore her own internal cues and follow yours. A key dynamic on the road to overweight and obesity, this clearly contradicts the recommendation only to eat for hunger's sake.

### Will Pee for Food

Nothing quite competes with potty training in giving parents a sense of
urgency to get their children to perform, whether it's pressure we put on ourselves, the rush to meet a child care mandate ("Your child can't move into the
next class until he's out of diapers."), or simply general societal expectations
("I taught my child to pee in the potty in less than a week before he was a year
old!"). That said, you'll find that many popular potty training regimens recommend offering your child M&Ms, ice cream, or a favorite dessert as a reward.
We've given this particularly tempting use of food a lot of thought, and we
keep coming to the same conclusion: Food is best left out of the bathroom
because when you resort to dishing out the treats morning, noon, and night
in return for some well-placed pee and poop, you're sending your child the
wrong message. Whenever possible, we therefore recommend that you stick
to nonedible forms of reward.

### Sugar-Free Bounty

Sweets are not the only thing you can use to encourage good behavior.
While the list of sugar-free options is endless, the effectiveness of any
reward is going to be highly dependent on what your child is particularly partial to. Some suggested alternatives to get you started include:

- Stickers. You can use a sticker chart, or simply let your child choose
  and collect them. Fortunately, they are both inexpensive and available
  in abundant supply.

- Tickets. For younger children, the reward of a ticket itself is enough
  motivation. Once your child gets older, you can offer actual tickets to
  a movie or other event, or decide to follow the example of the arcades
  and come up with some creative prizes for which your child can
  redeem her tickets.

- Books.

- Pencils (once they can be handled safely).

- Praise, hugs, and attention.

## Choosing Your Food Rewards Wisely

Whenever you deem it necessary to reward your child with a food treat for whatever reason, we suggest the following:

- **Keep It Few and Far Between.** If you find yourself unable to avoid the use of food as a reward altogether despite being aware of the implications, we suggest you allow yourself to do so only for those instances that occur infrequently, such as sitting still for a haircut or doing a good job at the doctor's office, rather than on a frequent basis ("If you eat your dinner, you can have dessert.").

- **Avoid an Overdose.** Avoid using food to reward the common behaviors that you expect your child to perform on a very regular basis, lest your child get far more than his fair share of sweets. Examples of these oft-rewarded behaviors include peeing in the potty, going to sleep without a fuss, eating one's meal, and "take this cookie and be quiet while mommy is on the phone."

- **Keep the End Result in Sight.** Don't forget to set an end date or a target result and then stick to it. Especially for behaviors that can take a good bit of time to accomplish, such as potty training, make it clear that once your child has mastered the skill, he will not continue to get Skittles indefinitely.

CHAPTER 18

# throwing food

**With the substantive change from** an all-liquid diet to one including solid foods comes the potential for your child's food to start flying. That's right, this chapter is all about throwing food, because from the day you add solid food to your baby's mealtime mix, you can expect your child to throw it. Granted, not all babies and toddlers throw their food, but the opportunity and likelihood are definitely there. And while many a parent finds the first noodle or spoonful of pudding gone astray to be cute and even picture worthy, the older kids get, the more likely it is that their far-flung ideas become a source of parental annoyance and embarrassment. It's messy, and with very few exceptions we can think of (a friendly game of egg toss or a flying shrimp at the hibachi restaurant where food is not only prepared at the table but tossed into your mouth come to mind), it does not fall into the realm of social acceptability. Given that food-throwing occurs for many reasons, we decided to take a step out of the ring and help you take into account why children throw food in the first place, and how you can teach them to keep both themselves and their food well grounded.

### Mealtime Milestones: The Developmental Milestones of Throwing Food

- **6 Months: Random Act.** At this age, babies are still learning to control and coordinate their movements and lack the fine motor skills of food handling that allow for precise pickup and delivery to one's mouth. While the startle (Moro) reflex that was responsible in past months for sending your baby's arms flailing is most likely to have subsided, babies at this age are nevertheless still prone to a bit of uncoordinated motion—whether it's with food in fist or not.

- 🍴 **9 to 12 Months: Reality Check.** By repeatedly giving her food the heave-ho, your child is deliberately testing 2 important principles: object permanence and gravity. This is the age of peek-a-boo—a game that relies on the concept of now-you-see-it, now-you-don't. Figuring out what happens to objects once they disappear and learning to anticipate their reappearance are big cognitive leaps, but when these principles are applied to food, the upshot is the not-so-charming problem of food over the edge of the high chair.

- 🍴 **15 Months: Taking Charge.** Fifteen-month-olds develop the ability to stack 2 items, want to feed themselves, and typically become more and more frustrated as their intentions exceed their abilities. As your child's food-handling involvement increases, so does the possibility that what's supposed to go up into her mouth will fall far short. Fortunately, this is also the age when kids learn to listen briefly and begin to follow simple commands such as "don't throw your food" and "put that down."

- 🍴 **18 Months: Throwing With Intent.** Simply put, toddlers throw because they can. At this age, your child is capable of throwing intentionally, and chances are her food (and your floor) will not be spared.

- 🍴 **2 Years: Overhand and Overboard.** Two-year-olds are ready, willing, and able to throw overhand, and are likely to have declared a distinct preference for using one hand over the other when tossing both balls and their food alike. Food throwing at this age can definitely get out of hand because it tends to be a matter of defiance and/or disinterest.

## Establishing Ground Rules

### *Look for a Motive*

Instead of getting immediately upset when food starts to fly, we always recommend that you first consider the motive. All too often we see inquisitive 9-month-olds taken to task for merely tossing aside their bottles, while flustered parents are all too quick to accommodate the calculated mealtime tantrums staged by their 2-year-olds. Figuring out your child's motive (if there is one) at any given mealtime will help you determine how best to handle the situation.

- **Accidentally Airborne.** Before taking any sort of swift action, keep in mind that it is entirely possible for food to be flung accidentally. Remember that mealtime mishaps are more common the younger the child is but can occur even after children are of the age when you'd think they would "know better" or should be capable of preventing them. At an age when kids are learning to hold their own, the food may fly but the sparks shouldn't. This form of food throwing does not warrant punishment, nor should you respond by removing your child from the table.

- **They've Lost That Hungry Feeling.** When children aren't hungry, they've had enough of whatever has been laid out before them, or their attention span has long since been exceeded, they're bound to come up with something novel to do with whatever food remains on their plates or trays. While you may ask from the vantage point of a mature adult, "Why throw it?"—in the hands of a young child, the temptation is to decide, "Why not?" Remember, social graces can take years to settle in. Until they do, you'd be well advised to learn to read the signs that your child has lost interest—*before* they include the spaghetti stuck to the wall or Cheerios scattered across the floor. Be consistent about what you will and won't tolerate, since this is how your child will ultimately learn to keep his food to himself. Instead, teach him a more contained way of communicating the fact that he's had enough, saying "All done!" or asking to please be excused. In the meantime, limiting your initial serving sizes can minimize the amount of ammunition remaining at the end of the meal.

- **Had a Bad Day.** On days when you know your child is crabby, tired, or especially if he's both, you might want to prepare to take cover. Even when ravenous, and even when it involves food they really, *really* like, toddlers have been known to take a stand and throw their food in a fashion that can best be described as cutting off one's nose to spite one's face. Although this may not be the best time to educate your child on the finer details of eating etiquette, you're going to want to make it clear that the show must not go on. Be unwavering in your approach by calmly but decisively disarming your child. If the situation doesn't improve, let mealtime be over and consider whether sleep rather than food might make things more peaceful and palatable the next time around.

- **Aiming to Please.** Whether you make a habit of laughing at your child's food-flinging antics or even if you happen to chuckle at them on one isolated occasion, either way he's sure to remember. It's a great indication of progress if you can relax enough to occasionally see the humor in some soaring solids and liquids, but if your toddler's flying food succeeds in amusing you, realize that it will buy you repeat performances.

- **Overt Manipulation.** It's definitely not beyond a toddler's grasp to figure out that throwing food can and all too often will get her both attention and whatever else it is she wants.

### Functional Food-Proofing

- **Keep the Food From Hitting the Fan…**and remember not to feed your child within a chicken nugget's throw of anything else that's going to be challenging to clean up. Tablecloths, placemats, curtains, and carpet are but a few of the more common household items that find themselves under this sort of friendly (or not-so-friendly) fire.

- **Cover Your Bases.** Consider covering the floor with a plastic floor protector, an old bed sheet, or even a drop cloth to help contain any fallen food. Anything that can be shaken out after meals, washed off (with a hose, if need be), or tossed in the washing machine will serve you well.

- **Dress Down for Success.** You can take a lot of the pressure to perform off everyone involved during mealtime by dressing down for the occasion. Favorite outfits shouldn't make their debut at mealtimes unless you are prepared for the resulting stains. We suggest that the clothes *you* wear should be able to withstand an occasional assault as well.

CHAPTER 19

# 5-second rule

**We have chosen to include the 5-Second Rule** as one of the nutritional challenges of parenthood in part to keep things lighthearted, but also because no one else seems to address it and we're sure that there are plenty of you out there who, like us, have been faced with the dietary dilemma of what to do with the cracker that's been thrown overboard or the grape that rolled away.

### The 5-Second Rule Defined

Just to make sure that we are all on the same page, let us first clarify what the 5-Second Rule actually is: It is a comforting notion that affords parents the opportunity to pick up and proceed as planned in serving food that has found its way to the floor. It is an often-cited yet unwritten rule standardly followed, joked about, and/or questioned by many. We can only assume that it came into being as a method of minimizing both tantrums and waste. Clearly, how you make use of (or scoff at) this "rule" will depend on several factors, not the least of which is your overall approach to cleanliness and how badly you or your child wanted the fallen food.

What's the dilemma? The question at hand is does this "rule" have any merit, giving you license to retrieve fallen food in good conscience? It may sound funny at first, but it is definitely a question that is commonly posed and rarely adequately answered. We decided it was high time that someone got to the bottom of it.

## Time for Trouble

Based on the very little information available on the subject, we have concluded that the 5 seconds you're allotted is completely imprecise and routinely adjusted to fit one's needs and allow determined parents sufficient time to complete the retrieval process. We've heard everything from 2 seconds for those with rapid response times to upward of 45—presumably for those who don't live life in the fast lane. And why not? Without knowing just how much time food can spend on the floor untainted and safely edible, applying this rule becomes a matter of pure convenience.

### Mealtime Milestone: Falling for Food

- **Now You See It, Now You Don't.** Sometime around 8 or 9 months, babies begin to test out a concept called object permanence and start to understand that objects exist beyond just what they can see. While playing peek-a-boo is a much anticipated and welcomed developmental milestone that lends evidence to this new skill, you're also likely to be faced with a lot more far-flung ideas on the food front as your child begins experimenting to see where food goes after it leaves her hands.

- **Easy Come, Easy Go.** Even older children drop food from time to time (OK…all the time). Whether as a result of less-than-perfect dexterity or part of an intentional outburst, we suggest you prepare yourself to deal with "dirty" food for the foreseeable future by accepting its inevitability and having a consistent plan on how to deal with it!

## Down for the Count

The best information we could find in the name of real science has to do with a study conducted by researchers at the University of Illinois who apparently took the time to investigate just how seriously we all should take the 5-Second Rule. What they found wasn't exactly sanitary: When it comes to bacteria sticking to food, there's no protective margin of safe exposure time. When your child's coveted gummi bear hits the ground, the potential microbial damage is done no matter how fast your retrieval reflexes may be—regardless of whether you're talking 2 seconds or 20.

From a contamination standpoint, that means no down for the count, no 3 strikes. It's an immediate out and replacement with a pinch hitter in the interest of hygiene.

Now before you vow to scorn every piece of fallen food, let us make one very relevant point: Children are guaranteed to spend quite a lot of time on the floor. And unless you have the unrealistic notion that you're always going to be able to keep your floor-crawling child's hands out of his mouth until they've been washed, it begs the question of what's the difference between having one's hands or one's food spend time on the floor before finding their way into one's mouth? The good news is that the types of germs found on a relatively clean kitchen floor are likely to pose less of a challenge to your child's intestinal tract than, say, those on the ground at the zoo. All things considered, we are therefore willing to admit that when it comes to certain circumstances and surfaces, we still believe in second chances.

CHAPTER 20

# read all about it!

**Do you ever find yourself getting tired** of the same old story day in and day out and having a hard time seeing the humor in your child's eating habits? We realize how trying it can be to have to translate and apply all of the many parenting recommendations every time you sit down to dinner, only to have your parental words of wisdom seem as if they're falling on deaf ears while being met with closed mouths. That's why we suggest you remember to table your discussions every once in a while and opt for the easy way out by stocking up on a few good children's books instead. The nutritional challenges of parenthood are universal enough that children's book authors have taken up the food fight cause on your behalf, and they have more than enough insight and humor to go around. Although you're sure to find many more once you know to start looking, we figured we'd start you off with a tempting baker's dozen.

1. *Eating the Alphabet*—**Lois Ehlert**
   - **Board book:** 28 pages
   - **Publisher:** Red Wagon Books; board edition (1996)

   It's colorful, it's built to last, and by just letting your child enjoy playing with the words boysenberry, okra, kohlrabi, and rhubarb, you'll be taking a big step in the right direction. After all, we know more than a few adults who couldn't begin to name a fruit or vegetable for each letter of the alphabet, much less bring themselves to eat them!

## The Developmental Milestones of Early Literacy

In the spirit of making both good eating *and* reading a part of every healthy childhood, the following is a book-related look at the well-defined developmental milestones of early literacy*.

- **Younger Than 6 Months: Never Too Young.** Unlike solid foods, it is never too early to start reading with your baby. Who cares if it's the sports page or Baby Bop—it will be the time you share together that counts, so have fun with it!

- **6 to 12 Months: Getting a Taste for Books.** Whatever babies are interested in at this age, they predictably put straight in their mouths. Books are no exception. Now that your baby can sit in your lap, grab for a book, and show her interest by batting at, turning, or gumming the pages, you'll find yourself especially appreciative of board books for their drool-proof nature.

- **1 to 2 Years: Becoming Routine.** As with food, your child will now figure out there's a lot more she can do with books than just put them in her mouth. As she makes a point of holding them, turning them right-side up, and carrying them to you to read time after time, you can start relating what's in her books to her real-life experiences—pointing to pictures and asking simple yet pointed questions like, "Where's the pea? Can you find the pea?" Before you know it, she'll be answering your questions, filling in the ends of each sentence, and reciting her VeggieTales back to you. As with meals, don't expect a long attention span, since it's the quality of the time spent that really matters, not the quantity.

- **2 to 3 Years: Read, Read, and Read Again.** Two-year-olds thrive on routine and love to master the power of predictability, so don't be surprised if yours is less than willing to try something new and instead wants to read the same story over and over (and over) again. If bedtime books have now become a habit—great! This is one habit you'll never need to break.

\* For more information, please visit www.reachoutandread.org.

2. *Yum—Harriet Ziefert*

- **Board book:** 20 pages
- **Publisher:** Blue Apple Books (2006)

*Yum* offers parents a perfect way to introduce both books and an array of healthy foods to those who are still as prone to putting their books in their mouths as they are their food. With 10 colorful and durable pages that put several basic shapes and foods on display for kids to chew on, this book is sure to start you out on the right track in making good reading and good eating appealing to your child long before he learns how to put up a fight.

3. *The Very Hungry Caterpillar*—Eric Carle
   - **Board book:** 26 pages
   - **Publisher:** Puffin Books (1994)

Each day, a very little and very hungry caterpillar eats his way through another piece of fruit, only to reach the end of the week still hungry. When Saturday rolls around, he eats his way through an impressive enough list of foods (one piece of chocolate cake, one ice-cream cone, one pickle, one slice of Swiss cheese, one slice of salami, one lollipop, one piece of cherry pie, one sausage, one cupcake, and one slice of watermelon, to be exact) that it leaves children entertained, the caterpillar with a stomachache, and parents with plenty to discuss. If you're looking to emphasize a moral to the story, we suggest sticking to what happens on Sunday, when the little caterpillar uses his better judgment, applies some restraint, and feels much better after eating just one nice green leaf. What follows is probably best applied to teaching your child about a caterpillar's life cycle rather than your child's eating habits, since the end of the story shows what was initially a little caterpillar turning into a "big fat" caterpillar before going on to become a beautiful butterfly!

4. *How Do Dinosaurs Eat Their Food?*—**Jane Yolen and Mark Teague**
   - **Hardcover:** 40 pages
   - **Publisher:** The Blue Sky Press (2005)

As a sequel to the award-winning *How Do Dinosaurs Say Good Night,* Yolen and Teague effectively excuse children from the table for this discussion of mealtime manners by inviting a disruptive dinosaur to dinner instead. No longer the center of attention, children can

chime in as these authors ask if a dinosaur should burp, blow bubbles in his milk, or stick beans up his nose at dinnertime. By the time you reach the end of the book, there will be no doubt left in your child's mind what this dinosaur needs to do to enjoy his food in a more socially acceptable way. In essence, you get to sit back and let the authors do your work for you. All you have to do is read as they introduce your child to the dos and don'ts of eating: everything from the concept of taking a "no thank you bite" to sitting still to saying please and thank you. No pressure, plenty of fun.

5a. *Green Eggs and Ham*—**Dr. Seuss**
- **Hardcover:** 72 pages
- **Publisher:** Random House Books for Young Readers (1960)

This is the ultimate food fight book. You may already know the story well enough to recite it in your sleep, but in the context of a food fight, it can be summed up like this: A pesky boy called Sam-I-Am tries his best to tempt a completely disinterested, nameless, and characteristically Seuss-like creature to taste his wares. After a full 13 increasingly outlandish but nevertheless failed attempts, it seems clear that no amount of coaxing is going to earn the boy's green eggs and ham the chance they deserve to prove themselves worthy of acceptance. But do not despair—this is a children's book, after all, and like Sam-I-Am, you and your child will know not to give up hope that there's going to be a happy end to this classic food-refusal story. Mr I-Do-Not-Like-Them *finally* decides to strike a deal and try them (if for no other reason than to be left alone), and lo and behold, he likes them after all. All we have left to say is boy, did that Dr. Seuss know what he was talking about!

5b. *Green Eggs and Ham Cookbook*—**Georgeanne Brennan**
- **Spiral-bound:** 64 pages
- **Publisher:** Random House Books for Young Readers (2006)

We've said it before, and we'll say it again—the more fun you can make of food, the better. While just about *everyone* has heard of

*Green Eggs and Ham,* not everyone puts as much thought into how to actually make them. If you haven't before heard of baking fresh fish with a Cheerio crust or Brown Bar-ba-loots' Truffula Fruits, you will now. With recipe ideas (such as "Schlottz's Knots" and "River of Nobsk Corn-off-the-Cobsk") derived from all 44 of Dr. Seuss' books, author Georgeanne Brennan has come up with a set of undeniably zany recipes that are sure to garner your child's interest while helping you add a distinctly fun flavor to your mealtime garnishes.

6.  *Froggy Eats Out*—**Jonathan London**
    - **Paperback:** 32 pages
    - **Publisher:** Puffin (2003)

    This book will give you a tadpole's view of what it's like to eat out at a restaurant meant for full-grown frogs. When Froggy's parents announce that they will all 3 be dining out at a fancy frog restaurant, Froggy and his parents do everything they can to get ready for the momentous occasion. Froggy even changes into clean underwear before hopping into his best pants, shirt, socks, and shoes, yet from the time they sit down at the candlelit table at the restaurant, it becomes increasingly clear that no amount of preparatory primping, scrubbing behind the ears, or repeated instructions to "be neat, be quiet, and don't put your feet on the table" can keep Froggy from almost turning his parents' anniversary dinner into a flop. Fortunately, these understanding frog parents figure out how to leapfrog their way to a compromise that leaves all 3 happily munching on burgers and flies.

7.  *The Berenstain Bears and Too Much Junk Food*—**Stan and Jan Berenstain**
    - **Paperback:** 32 pages
    - **Publisher:** Random House Books for Young Readers (1985)

    Although it may be quite literal, and Papa Bear may not be portrayed in such a great light (but then again, he never is), this book turns healthy eating into a family affair. It ranks as an all-time favorite in the

Jana household, even with Laura's husband! After indulging in quite a few too many Sugar Balls and Choco-chums, Papa Bear and the cubs find themselves bursting at the seams. Mama Bear decides that the family's bad eating habits have got to stop. What follows as the bears change their ways is nothing short of a course in nutritious eating, exercise, and health that comes appealingly disguised as yet one more beloved Berenstain book your child will want to read and read again.

8. *The Berenstain Bears Cook-It!*—**Stan and Jan Berenstain**
   - **Hardcover**
   - **Publisher:** Random House Books for Young Readers (1996)

OK, we admit it, recommending this book is a bit self-serving (since the subtitle is "Breakfast for Mama"). But if you look past what we consider to be the best part of the story—where Mama ends up with a well-balanced breakfast in bed as a birthday surprise prepared by her loving family—this book also illustrates what we firmly believe: Cubs (and kids) can really enjoy learning about foods by engaging in everything from their preparation to their presentation. Uncharacteristically in control of the situation, Papa Bear even remembers to introduce the cubs to some basic kitchen safety and cleanup in the process. Mama's meal is made complete only when Papa Bear and the cubs join her while she's eating and take turns telling about funny family events. This book is all about families sharing the best of the dining experience.

9. *Gregory, the Terrible Eater*—**Mitchell Sharmat**
   - **Paperback:** 32 pages
   - **Publisher:** Scholastic Paperbacks; reissue edition (1989)

According to his parents, Gregory is a terrible eater whose diet is revolting. He refuses to eat like a good little goat, and every time he sits down to dinner with his mom and dad, he knows he is in for trouble. Sound familiar so far? That's because author Mitchell Sharmat makes his underlying theme regarding coping with a picky eater as applicable to goats as it is to kids. Even if you and your child are having a hard time seeing eye to eye at the dinner table, you're sure to see the humor in this book—especially when you discover that what Gregory is pleading for (and what his parents insist is not fit for goat consumption) is fruits, vegetables, eggs, fish, bread, and butter. With some helpful advice from good old Dr. Ram ("[Picky eaters] need to develop a taste for good food slowly."), Gregory's parents learn to keep their cool, allow for compromise, and successfully restore peace (along with some old shoelaces hidden in a bowl of spaghetti) to the family table.

10. *How Are You Peeling? Foods With Moods*—**Saxton Freymann and Joost Elffers**
  - **Hardcover:** 48 pages
  - **Publisher:** Arthur A. Levine Books (1999)

  If you believe that food acceptance is at least in part based on how foods are presented then this book, along with any of the others in the authors' *Play With Your Food* collection including *Dog Food* and *Fast Food,* is for you. Making use of crisp photography, a huge dose of creativity, and a few well-placed beans (for eyes), Freymann and Elffers make their fruits and vegetables come to life. Whether teaching children about moods and feelings through the eyes placed convincingly on an orange or just having fun making a banana or artichoke look uncannily like man's best friend, when it comes to playing with food—these two take the cake. Read one or read them all and you will laugh out loud.

11. *Eat Your Peas*—**Kes Gray**
  - **Hardcover:** 32 pages
  - **Publisher:** Abrams Books for Young Readers (2006)

  We don't want to spoil the book by giving away the ending, but all you parents out there, be forewarned—if you can't take it, don't dish it out. This book not only exaggerates to the point of hilarity the lengths to which some parents are willing to go to get their kids to eat what's "good" for them, but it leaves no room for doubt that it doesn't matter one bite what you say but what you yourself eat that counts. After a single serving of *Eat Your Peas,* you'd better be prepared to adopt Strategy #7—Eat By Example on page 14.

12. ***Cookies: Bite-Size Life Lessons*—Amy Krouse Rosenthal**
    - **Hardcover:** 40 pages
    - **Publisher:** HarperCollins (2006)

Sometimes we get so wrapped up in discussions of what's healthy and where we want our children to fall on their growth curves that we forget that there's a lot more to food than how to get kids to sit at the table and what's listed on a label. Working off the theme that food has a much deeper meaning in our culture than what can be counted in calories, this book starts with a child and a batch of chocolate chip cookies and shows how in the process of mixing, baking, enjoying, and sharing something as simple as a cookie, our children can also learn a lot of bite-sized life lessons.

13. ***How to Eat Fried Worms*—Thomas Rockwell**
    - **Paperback:** 128 pages
    - **Publisher:** Yearling (1953)

If your child has you convinced that nothing could be worse than having to eat what you have set before him, it's time to check out this age-old book. After betting $50 that he will be able to eat 15 worms in 15 days, Billy must come up with ways to follow through. Even though *Fried Worms* is written at a second-grade reading level, it is a fun beginning chapter book to read aloud to kids well before they can read it to themselves. And if nothing else, it will serve you and your child a few useful reminders:

a)  Kids can get themselves to swallow just about anything they set their minds to.

b)  There really are much worse things you could suggest they eat than spinach.

c)  Ketchup really does come in handy in covering up the taste of just about anything!

CHAPTER 21

 brushing up

### A Behind-the-Scenes Battle

After dedicating a good part of each day to getting your child to eat well, drink responsibly, and be merry, we're willing to bet you're ready to put up your feet and call it a night. Yet even after all bedtime bottles and midnight meals have long been put to rest, we want to remind you of one last frequent and predictable nighttime battle: brushing your child's teeth. That's right, each night all of the dietary remnants of your child's day cling in hopes they will go undetected on your child's teeth. And even though your child's baby teeth are destined to fall out, cavities (which are really tooth infections) in baby teeth can lead to problems with the adult teeth that ultimately take their place.

### It Takes Two

Cavities are caused by a combination of sugar on the teeth and bacteria in the mouth. Eating a healthy diet and regular brushing can combat the sugar factor. Babies are born with normal "good" bacteria in the mouth and won't develop cavities, no matter how much sugar is on the teeth, unless "bad" bacteria take up residence in their mouths. Just where do these "bad" bacteria come from? They are most commonly transmitted from a parent's mouth (usually the mother's) to a baby's mouth by way of shared spoons, wetting a pacifier, or pre-chewing an infant's food. It is therefore recommended that you limit sharing saliva with your baby as best you can lest you share "bad" bacteria along with it.

As is the case with many common food fights, this one does not inherently have to pit you against your child. By starting out early—

when your child *wants* to put everything in her mouth—you can show her how to have fun brushing her teeth. In due course, you'll be able to stand watch as she learns to take over the task for herself. At the end of the day, you will have taught your child to take arms against a mouthful of potential troubles. The earlier you start, the more likely you are to win both your child's allegiance and the Battle of Decay.

### Mealtime Milestone: Taking Tooth Attendance

- **6 to 8 Months.** According to the books, the typical timeframe for teeth to make their debut is somewhere between 6 and 8 months. That said, teeth don't always appear by the book and have a habit of showing up unannounced months ahead of or behind schedule. With or without teeth, babies should have their first dental health checkup by their pediatrician as early as 6 months of age, and their first visit to the dentist anytime between the arrival of the first tooth and the first birthday.

- **1 Year.** Only a handful of children make it to their first birthdays without at least a couple, if not a mouthful, of teeth. That said, if your toddler's teeth are still nowhere in sight, do not fear: They're bound to show up sooner or later!

- **2 Years.** After your child turns 2 *and* is cooperative when it comes to spitting out on demand, you can start using small amounts of fluoride-containing toothpaste to brush your child's teeth.

- **2½ Years.** By the time most kids are 2½, they have a complete set of 20 teeth. Although these so-called baby teeth are considered by some to be mere stand-ins, how your child learns to care for them will have an impact that lasts far longer than the limited number of years they stick around before being replaced by a permanent set.

- **5 to 6 Years.** The typical age at which children begin to lose the first of their baby teeth.

**An Open and Shut Case**

It is next to impossible to get children to open their mouths when they don't want to. This holds true not only for getting them to eat—a food fight we've addressed elsewhere—but applies equally to getting them to open wide to brush. That's why we are such firm believers in starting early. When it comes to children and brushing, what you're really dealing with are 2 basic issues: (1) oral hygiene and (2) habit. And while we are aware that hygiene is not as much of an issue in the absence of teeth, we can assure you that most habits start young.

Long before teeth and toothbrushes enter the scene, children are known for sticking anything and just about everything into their mouths, and it is often what they do best. We strongly suggest you take full advantage of what is referred to as the "oral stage" of your child's development. While experts attuned to the challenges that lie ahead typically recommend brushing children's teeth as soon as they have them, we take things a step back and ask the question, "Why wait for teeth?" After all—if something is going to go into your baby's mouth, what better than a soft-bristled toothbrush that has been ergonomically designed for exactly that purpose with both safety and comfort in mind? Let him chew it. Let him suck on it. Use it to rub his gums. Bottom line: Clean gums aren't such a bad idea either, and the more your baby becomes accustomed to having a toothbrush in his mouth before he reaches the age of independence, the less likely you will be to have an open and shut case of toothbrushing refusal in your parenting future.

## Mealtime Milestone: The Age of Toothbrushing Independence

Although they're apt to try and convince you otherwise, children don't typically reach the age of independence when it comes to effective toothbrushing until somewhere between the ages of 6 and 10 years. Even though toothbrush and toothpaste packages may not explicitly say so, remember that the effective use of both really does require adult supervision.

### Let the Games Begin

Since it's going to be quite a while before your child masters toothbrushing for herself, we wanted to leave you with several practical suggestions to help you make it more fun and a matter of routine.

- **Start Early.** No teeth? No problem. Simply going through the motions still serves a very useful purpose.

- **Brush Often.** While we've focused thus far on bedtime brushing, technically speaking, your goal of brushing teeth is to clean food off of them, and the sooner the better. Yet few adults we know make a regular habit of brushing their teeth throughout the day. Start having your child brush after meals early in life and you stand a fighting chance of creating a lasting habit.

- **Sing, Sing a Song.** Or set a timer. Or come up with some other creative way to keep your child engaged in the act of brushing her teeth for the recommended 2 to 3 minutes, or for at least as long as it takes to make sure that your combined efforts leave them clean.

- **Check It Out.** If your child is showing signs of independence and insists on brushing on her own, then by all means let her. Just don't forget to get in the habit of proudly "checking out" her work at the end of each session while casually doing some touch-ups of your own.

- **Appeal to Taste.** If Cinderella, the Cat in the Hat, or a race car has better prospects of winning your child over than you do, then by all means, oblige. Feel free to indulge her tastes by letting her choose toothbrushes and toothpaste that she can really get excited about. For toddlers too young for toothpaste (see page 131), even the fluoride-free toddler toothpastes taste great and make it much harder for toddlers to resist opening their mouths.

- **Hands Off.** Right around the age when you're likely to start brushing, your child is likely to start grabbing. By giving her a soft-bristled brush (or 2) of her own to have and to hold, you will be able to avoid a fight over yours—leaving you well equipped to get the job done. Sure, it may take 3 toothbrushes instead of 1, but it's a small price to pay for a routine that really works.

- **Go Where No Child Has Gone Before.** We suggest you pay particular heed (and direct your child's attention) to those teeth that are most likely to be neglected. While you're helping her brush, describe what you're doing in terms she can relate to by pointing out her "biting" teeth (the chewing surfaces), her "smile teeth" (you guessed it—right in the front), and the tricky teeth in the back. Your goal—to teach your child to leave no plaque unturned.

### Toothpaste Temptations

Too much toothpaste can mean too much fluoride. Even though babies and toddlers are known to do more than their fair share of spitting food, they can't be relied on to spit out their toothpaste on demand. Since the fluoride found in toothpaste is clearly meant to be swished but not swallowed, current recommendations suggest waiting to introduce children to fluoride-containing toothpaste until they are *at least* 2 (although many kids don't learn how to spit effectively until much later). If you just don't feel right brushing without toothpaste, or if your toddler decides he must have some because he sees you using it, you do have the option of letting him use some fluoride-free toddler toothpaste until he learns to spit responsibly.

Even once he matures into a capable spitter, remind yourself (and your child) that the pretty swirls of toothpaste regularly shown on television have nothing to do with reality, and teach him to use a pea-sized amount at most. And lastly, be aware that the many tantalizing flavors of toothpaste—bubble gum, cinnamon, and orange mint to name but

 Too Much Fluoride

Ever since its introduction in the public water supply in the 1940s, fluoride has been heralded as a hero in the fight against cavities. However, the fact that *too much* fluoride has the ability to permanently change the appearance of one's teeth (a condition known as *fluorosis*) means you'll need to keep close tabs on how much your child gets, at least until you find that your child's swish-and-swallow has reliably become a swish-and-spit.

a few—have a way of tempting kids not only to brush their teeth, but to use a lot of it. When left to their own devices, some will even eat it. While fluoride is great for the teeth, it's not good for the tummy.

### Food and Flossing

The American Academy of Pediatric Dentistry recommends daily flossing as soon as 2 teeth are touching—something that in our experience can take years to occur. If your child expresses an interest in flossing her teeth long before they are even remotely close to making each other's acquaintance, don't squelch her enthusiasm. So what if she has gaps the size of your pinky finger? Seize the opportunity and teach her to floss away with ease in the name of supporting future healthy habits.

# PART V

# eating outside of the house

CHAPTER 22

# the friends and family feeding plan

**Given that you are taking the time to read this book,** we'll assume you're interested in developing a consistent approach to the food-related challenges of parenthood. We therefore feel compelled to discuss what may at times present itself as a sizable stumbling block: your automatic enrollment in what we call the Friends and Family Feeding Plan. What do we mean by this? Just that it can be difficult to feed one's children without feeling the "influence(s)" of one's loved ones.

Few people we know—even those who share the same genes, back-grounds, and/or traditions—share all the same attitudes and eating habits. We don't intend to suggest that nutritional input from those nearest and dearest to you is guaranteed to be more of a hindrance than a help, but it's a safe bet that the way you choose to feed your child is going to be met with occasional bad reception, and that you will be faced with at least a few friends and/or family members who don't subscribe to your plan. Somewhere along the way, you are likely to encounter casual observers, not to mention members of your own clan, who shake their heads and scrutinize how you handle your food fights—whether it is your commitment to ignoring your child's pleas for treats or your willingness to give yourself a break by giving in to them; whether you are the parent of a bottle-toting 2-year-old or have banned bottles altogether.

You name it—when it comes to food, friends, and family, everyone has their own way of doing things. You drop your eat-everything tod-dler off at grandma and grandpa's house for the weekend and next thing you know you're picking up a child with a preference for ice cream as his entrée of choice. Or you set up some play dates in hopes of teaching your child to play nicely and instead you learn that your neighbor's idea of an afternoon snack involves enough Oreos to guarantee he's got no appetite left for dinner. We realize that these sorts of dietary deviations can seem like a really big deal—especially for first-time parents trying to do the right thing. But from personal experience we know that in all but a few important instances, while a discussion may well be in order, fighting over what your friends and family feed your children is not worth the rift it stands to cause. While we don't have all the answers to this universal challenge (and we're pretty sure our own friends and family are going to be reading this chapter as well), we hope at least to give a little perspective on it and offer you a few considerations that may help you, your family, and friends break bread together without breaking bonds.

### Agree on the Terms

It's a good idea to think first about which food fights and feeding strategies you are most committed to and then share them with anyone who is involved in feeding your child. When you do, remember that the more you insist on things being done your way, the more difficult it will be for someone else to follow through. Imposing too many restrictive "because I said so" restrictions on friends and family without agreeing to disagree on at least some of them is sure to leave them feeling either incompetent, offended, or frustrated enough that they opt out of assuming the responsibility altogether. In the spirit of picking your battles, we suggest keeping your priority list short and presenting it as sweetly as possible.

- **Safety.** We hope this goes without saying, but we'll say it anyway. If someone responsible for feeding your child does not use the same level of caution as you do regarding such legitimate concerns as choking hazards and hot liquids, do not let brotherly love or the risk of hurt feelings keep you from insisting—or seeking alternate care.

- ⑂⑂⑂⑂ **Allergies.** Not everyone takes food allergies as seriously as they ought to. If your child has any food allergies, or if you have a strong family history and are avoiding certain foods as a precautionary measure (see "Allergies and Intolerances" on page 197), be sure to spell out what this means in the way of dietary restrictions. Also remember to let your friends and family know what to do in the event that your child accidentally eats an offending food.

- ⑂⑂⑂ **Deeply Held Beliefs.** Every parent we know has certain rules and routines to which they are particularly committed. If you're convinced that a single bedtime bottle will wreak havoc on future bedtimes or if you just can't stand the thought of your child eating pizza for breakfast or consuming food outside kitchen limits, it's perfectly acceptable to convey these wishes to those who carry the torch when you're not around. In this situation, just remember that others may not feel nearly as strongly as you do and your beliefs may not make sense to everyone.

### Establish Clear Lines of Communication

Food can prove to be a particularly touchy subject—especially because people tend to have strong opinions about it and may take any perceived criticism quite personally. It has been our observation that families and friends don't always communicate well to begin with, and in the context of food, we suggest you make it a point to bring any differences in opinion out into the open instead of letting them simmer. Otherwise, disagreements over something as trivial as how much syrup a child should be allotted on her pancakes or what her candy quota should be stand the distinct chance not only of ruining a visit, but potentially of affecting your overall relationship as well.

### Calculate Shared Mealtime Minutes

Take a moment to calculate just how many shared mealtime minutes you're actually talking about and then ask yourself how much influence your friends and/or family really stand to have in the grand scheme of things. Do they cause a departure from your child's dietary routine on a regular basis, or are the encounters few and far between? Sure, there will be times when it seems that years of hard work on the food front are going down the drain as quickly as your kids can wash down their chocolate cake with a can of cola, but if your permissive relatives live hundreds of miles away and only visit once or twice a year, you and your child's diet should be able to withstand that type of indiscretion far better than if they live next door.

### Try Not to Bite the Hands That Feed Your Children

We highly recommend taking a step back and considering the big picture before reacting too harshly. There are plenty of instances where we, as parents, find ourselves dependent on our friends and family to help watch and care for our children. And caring for them inherently involves feeding them. If you rely on friends and relatives, either tell yourself that you can recover where you left off and remember to be grateful for what they are offering, or find a way to take the task of feeding your children off their plates! That, or just give it up and be happy to have a little break from being master chef for your kids. Perhaps consider that you and your child may actually learn something and even benefit from the exposure to an alternative approach.

CHAPTER 23

# grocery shopping

**The introduction to the book** *The Mommy Myth* by Susan J. Douglas and Meredith W. Michaels begins like this: "It's 5:22 pm. You're in the grocery checkout line. …Your six-year-old is whining, repeatedly, in a voice that could saw through cement, 'But mommy, puleeze, puleeze' because you have not bought him the latest 'Lunchables,' which features, as the four food groups, Cheetos, a Snickers (bar), Cheez Whiz, and Twizzlers." Only 6 lines into the book and I (Laura) was laughing so hard I was crying. Of course, this all-too-common scenario is not nearly so funny when you find yourself in a similar situation. Well, you might as well brace yourself now, because carting a whining child through the grocery store has essentially become a parental rite of passage. After all, a toddler in the grocery store is like a kid in a literal *and* figurative candy shop. And if your child has tuned in to any television, he has almost surely been conditioned to recognize (and want) a vast array of advertised products that have been repeatedly paraded before him like commercial flashcards—most of which are for sugary or high-fat, unhealthy foods. You have several choices to consider carefully when it comes to how to handle your child's potential grocery-store whining, begging, pleading, and/or tantrums or, better yet, avoid this common food fight.

- **Keep on Carting.** This is the make-no-concessions approach to shopping-cart meltdowns. While not always easy to institute, it is usually very effective. All it really takes is the calm certainty that you are not the only parent who has walked the aisles with a wailing child. Sure, this is far easier said than done, but there will probably be more than a few parents who are eyeing you and your tantrum-throwing toddler—not in judgment, but out of respect for your resolve. What this resolve ultimately buys you is a shorter-lived problem. If you don't give in, your child will learn a whole lot quicker that it's not worth whining for Froot Loops, Fruity Pebbles, Fruit Roll-Ups, or any other type of fruity concoction that will never qualify for placement in the produce department.

- **Steer Clear of Temptation.** Have you ever noticed that the overall layout of most grocery stores is the same? The major food groups, or "whole" foods such as fruits and vegetables, grains, meats, and dairy tend to be displayed on the outer edges (or perimeter) of the store, while the processed foods are typically found in the aisles. Colorful produce and food that smells good—think bakery and deli—are often located near the front of the store to entice you to come in. This layout has definite benefits for the stores since these foods usually have the highest profit margins, but it also makes your shopping goals a bit easier: By "shopping the perimeter" (and avoiding candy-laden checkout lanes), you can effectively steer clear of many temptations and tantrums and come away with healthier and typically less-expensive fare.

- **Negotiate.** We don't want to mislead you—as committed as you may be to squelching your child's urge to whine, there may come a time when you find yourself compromising. And compromise is not always bad—especially in the instance when you stop to consider your child's request and decide that it really isn't so unreasonable after all. On the not-such-a-good-idea (but nevertheless a reality) side of things, you may find yourself giving in when you've had a rough day and just want the whining to stop. While we're all for the part about compromise and picking your battles in certain circumstances, be forewarned that negotiating for the sake of peace and quiet is going to guarantee you repeat performances. If you do choose to compromise, we strongly suggest doing so before you get in the store. If you are going to allow your child to indulge his wishes, be sure to clearly spell out in advance what it is he will be allowed to get, and then stick to this plan throughout the trip.

- **Avoid Running on Empty.** As adults, many of us have been cautioned not to go to the grocery store hungry lest our stomachs weigh in heavily on our decision-making. In other words, take hunger out of the shopping equation and you'll be far better equipped to resist temptation. At least to a certain extent, some (but not all) of your child's in-store demands may be hunger-dependent (see "Whining and Dining" on page 95), so it is worth trying to make sure he's well fed before going to the grocery store. Plain and simple: Hungry

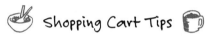 Shopping Cart Tips

Based on the fact that more than 24,000 children were treated in US emergency departments for reported shopping cart–related injuries in 2005—a majority of which involved either shopping carts tipping over or sudden falls that occurred *within* the presence of a watchful adult—you may want to consider alternatives to toting your kids around in shopping carts, such as the use of a stroller, wagon, baby carrier, or sling; getting your child to walk the aisles; leaving them at home with supervision; and even shopping online. If you do choose to cart your child, look for the kid-friendly carts that are low to the ground and often fashioned after fire trucks or race cars, and institute rules like those used on just about every amusement park ride we've ever been on.

- **Buckle Up.** All children should be securely buckled up before the ride begins.

- **Remain Seated.** Children should remain seated at all times.

- **In It for the Ride.** No one is to ride on the outside of the cart or the ride will come to an immediate halt.

- **Keep Contained.** All hands and feet are to be kept inside the cart at all times.

- **Drive Responsibly.** Only responsible adults should be in charge of operating the ride.

children tend to be crabby children, and crabby children are not only more inclined to beg indiscriminately for any and all of the junk laid out before them, but they tend to whine a whole lot louder.

- **Say Your Goodbyes.** A lot of parents have told us that when their child starts begging and whining for things he can't have at the grocery store, they simply pick him up, turn around, and leave. From a behavior management standpoint, this sends a clear message and helps children learn consequences. By all means feel free to do this if you can't get past the feeling that a walk down the aisle with a wailing child is nothing short of a walk of shame. But if you ask us, it's an even greater shame to leave without the food you came for in the first place and it also stands to send your child the message that he gets to call the shots.

- **Go It Alone.** You may soon find that, as a parent, a solo trip to the grocery store is only one stop short of a day at the spa, especially if your child happens to be going through his whining stage. Rest assured that it is not a cop-out to find a convenient time (such as naptime, early morning, or after bedtime—whatever suits your family's schedule) and/or somewhere safe to leave your child—at a friend's, a babysitter's, or with your spouse—while you stroll the aisles at your leisure. If you're really lucky, you may even find a friendly neighborhood grocery store such as Wegmans, Price Chopper, or ShopRite where we have heard that child care is actually made available to parents while they shop.

CHAPTER 24

# 🍴 child care cuisine

**Teaching children healthy habits needs to start** at home, and figuring out how to avert food fights within the confines of your own kitchen is a very good place to start. But it shouldn't end there. Not when eating out on a regular basis has become routine for nearly 2 out of every 3 children younger than 5 years in the United States. Contrary to what you may by thinking, we're not just talking about restaurants. We're referring to the many kids who eat and drink without any parental supervision each day in child care centers across America. As we finish our discussion of eating outside of the house, we want to focus some much-needed attention on the often-overlooked challenges—as well as the potential benefits—of child care cuisine.

### 🍜 We Really Care A Lot ☕

Child care is a place where children can go when their parents work, attend school, or need to attend to things that are not appropriate or convenient with children in tow. Regardless of the reasons, the more time children spend in child care, the more their eating habits stand to be influenced by what they eat and drink while they're there. Recent data suggest that almost 12 million of our country's children younger than 5 years spend some portion of every week in the care of someone other than their parents, and those who have working mothers spend an average of 36 hours a week in child care.

### What Child Care Stands to Offer

If feeding children at home were always easy, there would be no need for this book. In many ways, the challenges of feeding children in the child care setting really aren't all that different. Yet there are several defining features of child care that, in an *ideal* setting, are particularly good for promoting the principles of healthy eating.

1. **Peer Pressure.** Nowhere does *positive* peer pressure stand to be more beneficial or easier to implement on a regular basis than in child care programs where children are served the same foods as their peers and are encouraged (but not forced) to try them. Nothing convinces a picky eater to taste something new like watching all of her friends sit down and dig in. No parental demands, no pressure, and usually no other options.

2. **What You See Is What You Get.** Having no other options is key. At home, parents often succumb to the temptation of short-order cooking and are quick to offer alternative foods. This is an option that is much less feasible in the context of child care. When children discover there's no room for negotiation and they can either eat what they are served or be hungry, they are far more likely to try new foods, eat according to hunger, and skip the complaints.

3. **Familiarity Breeds Content.** We have found that parents—including us—often don't handle rejection all that well, especially at the dinner table at the end of a long day. When children refuse to eat something, it can be tempting to accept 1 or 2 food refusals as their final answer instead of reminding ourselves that it can take 10 to 15 exposures to a new food to be won over...or at least be content with it. The fact that the same menu items are often served on a regular basis in child care results in children being repeatedly exposed to a variety of foods regardless of their initial reactions. If they don't like cottage cheese or lasagna the first time around, no problem. They'll be afforded plenty of additional opportunities to become better acquainted.

4. **A Set Schedule.** Consistency of mealtime routines can be a key to establishing a healthy approach to eating. In child care, regularly scheduled meals and snacks are often mandated by state licensing regulations. Another advantage to having clearly defined times

for meals and snacks is that children are less likely to eat and drink continuously throughout the day.

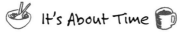

### It's About Time

The following are several relevant guidelines regarding the recommended timing of daily meals and snacks for children in child care.

- Children who spend 8 hours or less in child care should be offered at least 1 meal and 2 snacks or 2 meals and 1 snack while they're there.
- If they will be in child care for more than 8 hours, children should be offered at least 2 meals and 2 snacks or 1 meal and 3 snacks.
- Toddlers and preschool children can't be expected to sit for too long. Time spent at the table should range from 10 to 20 minutes for meals, and 5 to 15 minutes for snacks.
- A nutritious snack should be offered to all children mid-morning and mid-afternoon.
- Children should be offered food every 2 to 3 hours except when they are asleep.
- Infants' nutritional needs may require that they be fed more frequently than every 2 hours.

5. **Family-Style Meals.** Given that the hectic pace of our parenting lives has made it increasingly difficult to set aside protected time for family meals at home, the opportunity for children to sit down to dine with friends and, ideally, caregivers on a daily basis is a particularly advantageous feature of eating in child care. Caregivers can be excellent role models when they eat with the children, eat the same food as the children, practice good hand washing, teach table manners, and talk about trying new foods in positive ways.

### Child Care Checklist

Some child care programs have a set menu provided by the company they work for. Others have food catered in, or they ask parents to pack their own food. Some have a cook who prepares home-style meals, just in larger quantities. There are pluses and minuses to all situations.

Find out what the deal is in any child care program you are considering by both asking and observing. While you're sure to find useful checklists designed to help you evaluate your child care options, most unfortunately include only a question or two on this important subject. Given the fact that the nutritional aspects of child care are equally as important as class size, teacher-to-student ratios, safety, and curriculum, we've suggested some additional considerations below to help make your search for quality care more fruitful.

### At the Very Least

Every state except for Idaho, which does not license child care centers, requires that meals and snacks served in child care meet minimum nutritional standards. You can find out what your state's licensing requirements are by contacting your local child care licensing agency or by checking out the National Resource Center for Health and Safety in Child Care and Early Education Web site at http://nrc.uchsc.edu/STATES/states.htm. This Web site identifies the licensing agencies and posts all child care regulations for every state. Once you know what is required, you can figure out if child care programs in your area are meeting these minimum requirements.

- **At Your Service?** In states where food service is not mandated, parents are more likely to have to pack their own—an added responsibility that we find often gives way to time constraints and convenience and results in children being fed far more packaged, processed foods than is good for them. If, on the other hand, the food provided in child care is not nutritious and little thought is given to variety or balance, you may well want to retain control if given the option.

- **What's the Fare?** The potential benefits of regular meals, peer pressure, and learning to eat what's been served are all lost if unhealthy foods and drinks dominate the child care menu. If food is provided, ask to see the menu. Not only should meals and snacks be planned out ahead of time, but you'll also want to make sure that what's on the menu is actually being served, and that it fits your overall nutritional agenda.

- **Is There Restricted Entry?** Share and share alike is not always a good philosophy when it comes to food in child care—especially if food that is brought in by other parents is not closely monitored for choking hazards, allergenic foods, or far less nutritious fare than what you bargained for. That's why it's a good idea to ask if there are rules in place about bringing in food from the outside for snacks, meals, and special occasions.

- **The Size Is Right?** Are children given enough or too much food? Can they ask for more if they are hungry? Licensing standards typically define what should be considered age-appropriate serving sizes for the foods and drinks provided in child care. Check to see not only if children are being served adequate amounts, but also if there's any limit on how much they get in order to keep kids from having fourths and fifths of favored foods while eating none of the ones they deem less desirable.

### Peanut-Free Providers

Some child care centers, including the one that Laura owns, now have No Peanut policies in place to significantly limit the potential for peanut exposure. This can prove to be an unexpected challenge when bringing in holiday or birthday treats: While sugar cookies and cupcakes don't often contain peanuts themselves, if you read the label carefully you'll find that many are made in the same bakeries or factories where peanut products are prepared.

- **On the Alert?** If your child has any food allergies, be sure to find out if her caregiver is able to adequately accommodate any dietary restrictions, and discuss what precautions are in place to ensure that your child won't inadvertently be fed an offending food.

- **Would You Like Some Juice With That?** Juice seems to have long since established itself as the drink of choice in child care. It is frequently served despite the fact that there's really no inherent need for it, since serving milk with meals and water with snacks makes for the perfect mix of drinks. In part, the pervasive presence of juice may be the result of the common licensing requirement that 2 food groups be served at every sitting—a regulation intended to make certain that children are fed nutritious fare in child care. While juice is not considered to be a nutritionally sound substitute for serving actual fruits, it is nevertheless frequently poured into children's cups as a way of fulfilling this requirement (see A Juice Box on page 81 of "A Revealing Look at Pop Culture").

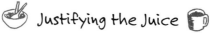

### Justifying the Juice

If your child care provider serves juice, make sure that it:

› Is 100% juice

• Doesn't entirely replace fruit on the menu

• Doesn't exceed 6 ounces a day for children between the ages of 6 months and 6 years

• Doesn't flow too freely. Children should not be allowed to sip throughout the day.

• **How's the Hygiene?** While exposure to germs is admittedly a fact of life in child care, when making your rounds, check that your child care provider's hygiene habits are as good as, if not better than, what you follow at home. Remember to take a look at where food is prepared and eaten. Are the kitchen, the dishes, and the tables clean? Is there someone trained in food handling? Are the hands of the cook, those involved in serving, and the children routinely washed before they reach for the food that's placed in front of them?

### Partner With Your Provider

If you're otherwise happy with your child care setup, but you find that the approach to nutrition leaves something to be desired, remember that feeding children and instilling healthy eating habits is a work in progress. Use this information as an opportunity to talk with your child's caregivers about how they stand to contribute to the cause and what improvements you'd like to see. For more information on healthy practices in child care, see www.healthykids.us/chapters/meals_main.htm.

CHAPTER 25

# ⑪⑪⑪⑪ tv dinners

**Let's just assume for a minute that you** now consider yourself sufficiently armed to take on one of the most pervasive of the contemporary parenting food fights. Then imagine we were to ask you to close your eyes, sit down, and prepare to face this formidable foe. Open your eyes and what do you think you'd find? No, the answer is not spinach. Would it be free-flowing soda pop, boxes upon boxes of sugar cereals, and candy galore? A Mighty Kids Happy Meal followed by a long line of Lunchables? Well, sort of. That's because the foe we're referring to has the distinct ability to change its stripes and be any or all of these food fight challenges all at once. It is an outside influence so strong that over the past 50 or so years, it has invaded just about every home in America and wreaked havoc on many a mealtime. Perhaps the most disturbing part of what we're about to tell you is that we are talking about something that may well be a marauder disguised as one of your most prized possessions. We hate to be the bearers of bad news, but were you to open your eyes and see the light, you'd find yourself looking straight at your television set.

### Tuning In to the Facts

Consider for a moment the following statistics about just how engrossed our country's children have become in television.

- A whopping 8 out of 10 children younger than 6 years spend at least 2 hours a day watching television, playing video games, and/or using the computer.

- Televisions in kids' bedrooms have become the norm: As many as 1 in 5 *toddlers* younger than 2 years is estimated to have one in their bedroom.

- Two-thirds of children between the ages of 6 months and 6 years watch television every day, according to a recent Kaiser Family Foundation survey.

No way of looking past it—television sets are everywhere and our children are watching them. And while some speculate that time spent watching television can be related to everything from poor sleep habits and bad grades to a sedentary lifestyle, it is what comes between the regularly scheduled programming—the television ads themselves—that many experts feel can have one of the most profound effects on your child's nutritional health and overall well-being.

**Marketing Milestone: The Development of a Consumer**

Just as television content programmers look for ways to attract young viewers, so do the television advertisers. As much as we strive for originality, we are most certainly not the only ones to have caught on to the fact that food habits and preferences start early in life. In advertising terms, your child is a great deal more than just an impressionable child: She is an up-and-coming consumer. And in much the same way as we have devoted our careers as pediatricians to gaining a better understanding of children and their development, so too have the retailers and marketers of the world. As we looked more closely at how our children have become the targets of much attention, we came across this actual list of developmental marketing milestones and wanted to share with you a side of your child's development of which you may not be aware. Be forewarned: Some readers may find the following milestones to be particularly disturbing.

- **Age 1: The Age of Observation.** At the same time that children are learning to sit up, talk, and start to communicate their wishes, they are also spending ample amounts of time strapped in shopping carts and strollers exploring the colorful wonders of the marketing world around them while their parents shop.

- **Age 2: The Age of Getting What They Want.** Two-year-olds get smart to the fact that what they see on television is actually available on store shelves and theirs for the asking. Given that it is a 2-year-old's job to figure out how to get what it is she wants using whatever means necessary—whether that be hitting, screaming, or otherwise throwing tantrums—marketers can rely on these growing persuasive abilities as a reliable means to a purchasing end.

 Tricks Are for Kids

If only all parents were aware of just how many tricks of the marketing trade are routinely employed in the 40,000 ads their children see each year, we're willing to bet that far fewer 2-year-olds would be allowed to get their nutritional advice from the likes of SpongeBob and Scooby-Doo. There is no question that food advertising influences a child's food choices. What makes marketing to kids so successful? An integral part of the process is a ploy known to marketers as the nag factor. While just about all parents we know spend a considerable amount of time trying to teach their children not to whine, there are people out there who are actually paid to *encourage* your child to do just that; because with enough pestering, it is a well-recognized fact that parents are likely to give up and give in (see "Whining and Dining" on page 95). Just remember that although it's only natural for kids who watch television commercials to want what they have seen, it's your duty to interject some good judgment and make sure they learn that they can't always get what they want!

- **Age 3: The Age of Selection.** Even before they are clear on their ABCs and 123s, children can readily recognize brands and help their parents retrieve them from the local stores—an eagerly anticipated milestone in the minds of the marketers.

- **Age 4 and Older: The Age of Independent Purchasing.** Whether first accompanied by a parent or ultimately wielding purchasing power of their own, kids typically blossom into independent buyers as early as the ripe old age of 5—often before they've even graduated from kindergarten.

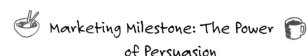

### Marketing Milestone: The Power of Persuasion

Experts suggest that until the age of 8 or 9, kids aren't good at distinguishing the persuasive promotional efforts of advertisements from reality, nor are they adequately equipped to evaluate commercial claims.

## Learning to Control Your Child's Media Diet

Now that you are more aware of the nutritional hazards of television, we want to take a look at a few practical strategies for controlling your child's media diet. First, let us be clear—we are not extremists, and we do not believe in throwing the baby out with the bath water. But we do think it is prime time for all of us to take some careful measures.

### Tuning It Out

You really do have complete control. By keeping the television turned off or out of your home, the television ads so carefully crafted with your child in mind can't touch them. Yes, we realize it is easier said than done, but it is nevertheless worth saying.

### Media Matters

The American Academy of Pediatrics recommends *no* television for children younger than 2 years and no more than 2 hours a day of total media time (television/videos, computer, video games, etc) in the years to follow.

### Turn to Tapes

Videotapes, DVDs, and even TiVo for tots. By using any of a multitude of prerecorded and prescreened options, you can help to ensure that (a) what your child watches meets with your approval and is of some educational value, (b) you more easily set clear limits on your child's viewing time, and (c) you can filter out any unwanted attempts at advertising.

### Offer Limited Programming

Set clearly defined limits both on the time and the type of programming your child is allowed to watch, and stick to them.

### Stop Buying the Idea of TV Dinners

Back in 1954, a Swanson executive was faced with a problem. He had 270 tons of leftover Thanksgiving turkeys. Inspired by the divided plastic trays used by the airlines at the time, he reportedly arranged for 2-dozen women to scoop turkey, corn bread, gravy, buttered peas, and sweet potatoes into what then became known as the first TV dinners. Having grossly underestimated the demand, Swanson proceeded to sell 10 million of them that year. Although they stopped calling them "TV Dinners" in 1962, the concept of dining in front of the television has unfortunately carried on throughout the decades. We especially recommend keeping mealtimes television-free. And while you're at it, we suggest you make it a point to keep your child from getting into the habit of eating while watching during *or* between any and all meals.

### Stay Tuned In

Be aware of what your child is watching on television—not only the shows themselves but what comes before, after, and everything in between. While it is beyond the scope of this book for us to discuss the kid-inappropriate nature of *CSI* or even the nightly news, suffice it to say we are advocates of significantly limited viewing. Even when your child is watching kid-friendly programming, you will still want to shield him from the barrage of intervening advertisements that flood the airwaves, not to mention keep them (and better yet, the television set) out of his bedroom.

CHAPTER 26

# ⫶eating out without reservations

**It used to be that eating out at a restaurant was reserved** for special occasions and usually involved a table for 2, a white tablecloth, and leaving the children at home with a sitter. But not so anymore. If yours is like most families today, eating out has become a way of life. In the last 10 years, Americans have been dining out in droves—spending roughly half of their families' total food budgets and consuming nearly a third of all calories away from home.

Along with this convenience-driven movement comes the added pressure of getting our children to perform. It is generally easier to treat the task of teaching children healthy, safe, and socially acceptable eating habits as a work in progress in the privacy of your own home. At a restaurant, however, your family's mealtime matters will be on exhibit, and your child's diet, his developing dining skills, *and* your patience are much more likely to be put to the test.

With this in mind, we have taken the liberty of ordering for you our top 10 tips to help keep your child's eating habits from turning into frustrating public displays of disaffection and make your family's meals out on the town more enjoyable for everyone involved.

1. **Maintain a Healthy Attitude.** Eating out requires a lot of social skills—skills that children must not only be taught, but be given the chance to practice. Each time you head out to a restaurant, be sure to remind yourself that being quiet and sitting still with one's napkin across one's lap throughout an entire meal doesn't come naturally.

2. **Pick a Restaurant That Caters to Kids…**at least when you're first getting started in order to take some of the pressure off. How do you know a family-friendly restaurant when you see one? Just conjure up an image of a romantic candlelit dinner and then look for the complete opposite. If there's a "Kids Eat Free" sign in the window, the hostess is ready and waiting with a box of crayons, and the level of background noise is high enough to drown out any unexpectedly loud outbursts, it's a safe bet you're good to go. Don't forget that as your child's mealtime manners develop, you can look forward to dining at restaurants that cater to a more mature crowd.

3. **BYOB.** Although the stress of eating out at a restaurant can certainly leave some parents feeling like they could use a drink, this BYOB recommendation has nothing to do with alcoholic beverages. Instead, it is a reminder to bring your own *backup.* Bringing along a couple of mealtime accessories can go a long way toward making the meal go smoothly and helping your child enjoy rather than ruin the ambiance.

   • **Food.** It is perfectly acceptable to bring along some food for your child, just so long as you don't rely so heavily on the bring-your-own approach that you miss out on your child's golden opportunity to try new things. This option is best reserved for times when you know your child is unlikely to be able to tolerate the wait, for infants who have not yet taken to table foods, and for particularly picky toddlers.

   • **Toys for Tots.** When faced with a wait, a couple of books and a quiet toy or two can work wonders in helping to more peacefully pass the time—especially if they're ones your child has not seen before. For babies, this may be as easy as supplying a rattle or rubber-tipped spoon, while for older children, a piece of paper and a few crayons is often all it takes to paint a prettier picture.

- **Accessories.** Bring bibs and bottles in particular, but if you're headed to a restaurant that doesn't provide cups with lids, a sippy cup might also be in order.

4. **Keep in Mind That It's About Time.** Many of the problems children have behaving in restaurants can be traced back to having too much time on their hands. Boredom and impatience are not your friends. The longer children are expected to be on their best behavior, the more likely they are to become restless—especially if they have nothing to keep them occupied. Since the clock will be ticking from the minute you walk in the door, we recommend:

   - **Calling Ahead.** Make reservations or take advantage of call-ahead seating to increase your chances of being seated at a table rather than in the waiting area when you arrive.

   - **Going Early.** By beating the rush, you'll be less likely to have to wait for a table, service will hopefully be faster, your child will probably be less tired and crabby, and those seated around you will most likely be other families with young children who have exactly the same idea in mind.

   - **Ordering Efficiently.** On those days when you're running short on time or patience, skip the formality of ordering drinks first and get your full order in the first chance you get. If you're anticipating the need for a quick getaway, you might even request the check be brought out with the meal.

5. **Clear Your Own Table.** We realize that one of the clear-cut benefits of dining out is that you aren't responsible for the cleanup afterward, but we're actually talking about clearing the table *before* you eat. That's because restaurants are seldom childproof to the extent necessary to keep your meal accident-free. As soon as you sit down to dine, remember to scan the table for items that stand to disrupt your dinner and make sure they don't fall into the wrong hands. We've listed a few of our personal favorites to get you started.

- **Candles.** No explanation needed, except to point out that kids seem to be drawn to candles like moths to light, and if you let your child play with them, he's playing with fire.

- **Sharp Knives.** They are often put at every place setting around the table with complete disregard for the age of the person who is to be seated there. You'll want to make sure you're the first to grab for them. In fact, if your baby or toddler is not yet skilled in the use of utensils in general and is more likely to bang a fork and spoon then eat off of them, you'd be wise to grab those too.

- **Sugar and Spice.** While children rarely end up getting hurt while shaking the salt or playing with the packets of sweetener, a spoonful of sugar spread across the table does nothing to help the meal go down.

- **Drinks.** Even though spills are to be expected, they still tend to put a damper on the dining experience. You don't need to stop ordering drinks—just make sure that they aren't set at your child's elbow or precariously perched too close to the edge of the table, and that they come with lids whenever they're available.

6. **Don't Just Say No.** Regardless of what sort of socially challenging show your child is putting on, be aware that just saying no, with no teaching and no ramifications, has been shown to be of little use. Before you even go out, discuss what you expect of your child and what the clearly defined consequences will be if he is unable to behave during the meal. Whatever you choose to use as a consequence, just make sure you're willing and able to follow through—even if that means leaving the restaurant well before dinner has been served (see Tip #10).

7.   **Take a Healthy Approach to Kids' Meals.** Restaurants offer a great opportunity to expose children to new foods and flavors, but they also run the real risk of serving as an excuse to check your nutritional goals at the door. According to one survey, the top 5

most popular foods ordered at restaurants by children younger than 6 years were french fries, chicken nuggets, pizza, hamburgers, and ice cream. This leads us straight to the topic of kids' menus. No doubt about it, ordering off the kids' menu can make your overall dining experience easier. The problem is that kids gravitate toward food they're familiar with, and they quickly learn to order *only* off the kid's menu—an ordering pattern that often becomes firmly entrenched and ensures that almost 100% of their entrées will consist of a very narrow range of not-so-healthy foods. Whenever possible, we suggest swapping out fries for a healthier side, skipping the free refills on soda altogether and ordering milk instead, and encouraging your child to broaden his horizons by looking beyond the confines of the kids' menu and giving him the chance to taste foods off of your plate as well.

8. **Contain Costs.** Part of the temptation to let children order off the kids' menu stems from the fact that it is almost always less expensive. For less than the cost of an entrée, you can often get your child a main course, a side dish, a drink, and a dessert. That said, kids' menus rarely offer a good deal when it comes to nutrition. We therefore suggest giving the following alternative cost-containment measures a try as well:

   • **Share and Share Alike.** To give your child exposure to a wider range of food choices while giving your wallet a break, consider sharing an adult entrée. This works particularly well if your child has a small appetite and your own entrées routinely go unfinished, or you have more than one child so they can share amongst themselves.

   • **Downsize.** Ask if you are able to order your child a scaled-down serving of an adult-sized entrée at a reduced price. Appetizers can also double as less-expensive kid-sized entrées. Just be sure to check first to see if the appetizer section is dominated by fried and fatty foods.

- **Two for the Price of One.** Avoid the natural temptation to teach your child that he needs to clean his plate just because you paid for it (see The Clean Plate Club on page 89). Especially with the oversized portions often served up in restaurants, take the approach of encouraging your child to eat only what he's hungry for, and then take the rest home to serve at a later date. As an aside, this is a strategy that works as well for adults as it does for children.

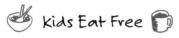

## Kids Eat Free

It's a safe bet that "kids eat free" means that a restaurant not only welcomes families, but that you can save a considerable amount on your final bill. Be aware that this deal typically applies to those days of the week when business tends to be slower (such as Tuesdays and Wednesdays), and that many restaurants only offer one free kid's meal per full-fare adult.

9. **The Tipping Point.** Unless you have everything under such control that taking your child to a restaurant leaves no more mess and requires no more service than if you were dining solo, we highly recommend adjusting your tip accordingly. As a rough rule of thumb, your tip should be proportionate to the quality of family-friendly service you receive, the number of extra trips your server has to make to and from your table to accommodate your family's needs, *and* the amount of mess you leave in your wake.

10. **The Take-Home Message.** According to the head of the National Restaurant Association, restaurants have always served as a social oasis for friends and family to enjoy quality time together over a relaxing and rewarding dining experience. We aren't sure whose family he was referring to, or the ages of those at the table, but it's unrealistic to expect an oasis, or even a relaxing meal, each time you head out to a restaurant. There will be days when positive attitude, advanced planning, and practice will pay off. But there are sure to

be others when nothing is going to be enough to avert a restaurant meltdown. If and when you find yourself with a child who is too tired, too impatient, or too determined to break the sound barrier to sit quietly in his seat, it's time to call it a night and try again later. In the meantime, you can always order takeout and practice at home. In doing so, you will join the ranks of most Americans who order more takeout meals than eat in the actual restaurants.

CHAPTER 27

# plane and simple: in-flight food fights

**Let's face it—flying with kids can really be quite a trip.** Given that there's almost nothing more stressful than traveling with a hungry infant or child and finding yourself at the mercy of delays, detours, or missed connections (not to mention an inadequately stocked food service cart), it's no wonder that air travel has a way of elevating issues of food and drink to a status far beyond what they might otherwise attain. After all of the preparatory purchasing, packing, and pre-boarding involved, it's easy to forget to factor in food and drink. While you might get lucky and make it through to your final destination just fine without any food fore-thought, it's better not to leave things quite so up in the air, since a little planning can go a long way toward preventing turbulent travels.

> ### Time Your Travels
>
> While in your pre-parenthood days you may have tried to avoid long layovers, if not passed them up altogether in favor of direct flights, consider the fact that having time in the airport to sit down for a meal can often make the rest of the trip a breeze. This may be more easily said than done, but try to schedule food into your timetable.

As far as nutrition goes, unless your children are extremely frequent fliers, a few dietary indiscretions during air travel really shouldn't be cause for concern, nor should they justify a battle. The way we see it, you have 2 choices: You can either adjust your rules regarding what and when your child is allowed to eat and drink in order to fit the circumstances, or you can stay your nutritional course—a decision that will require a more carefully constructed flight plan (and a more fully stocked carry-on).

### Anticipate Air-Conditioning

There's nothing quite like a service cart making its way down the aisle of an airplane to elicit a conditioned response: Someone kindly offers your children something to eat or drink, and they take it. It doesn't matter if they're actually hungry or thirsty. It doesn't matter if it's well past bedtime and they've already eaten more than a day's worth of meals. And of course, any nutritional caution you typically use may well be thrown to the wind in the name of availability and the out-of-home experience. Though faced with a potential deviation from their normal routine, the good news is that it is not that difficult to teach children to curb this instinct not only at home, but when they take to the air as well.

### Beverage Service Basics

At home, your toddler may go hours without drinking. But book a flight and you may find that your child claims to be so parched that an hour layover or having to wait for beverage service suddenly becomes analogous to crossing the Sahara desert. While the situation is rarely this extreme, the tendency toward excessive drinking on airplanes does have some extra parenting implications that are well worth mentioning. As with any sort of effective approach to parenting, we suggest that you lay down a few key drinking ground rules before taking off.

- **Drink Selection.** We have noticed that the healthier drink selections such as milk and water don't exactly fly off the beverage carts. In fact, some flights don't even carry milk. And while airlines often do offer juice and/or fruit drinks alongside the ever-abundant soda pop selections, in the end they all count as sugary drinks your child is likely to find hard to resist. We therefore suggest that you decide ahead of time (a) what your child is going to be allowed to drink and (b) how much.

> ### 🥣 Hydrating Needs on Airplanes ☕
>
> One of the reasons that some parents are so quick to keep the fluids flowing both for themselves and for their children may be based on the assumption that airplanes cause dehydration. Because the humidity level on airplanes is typically less than 20%—a level that rivals conditions found in the desert—the reason for the dry lips and dry skin that routinely occur during air travel is usually a factor of dry *air,* not an overall lack of fluid intake. Our advice: It's OK to drink up, but there's no need to overdo it!

- **Smart Sipping.** The freestanding plastic cups ubiquitous to airplanes run the risk of sabotaging your child's attempts at neat sipping, even before you factor in any turbulence or bumped trays. Their slightly raised rims have a way of making even the most skilled drinkers dribble, and they usually don't come with lids. We would therefore like to propose that airplane travel is the perfect time to offer young children sippy cups. If your child is already past the sippy cup stage and you don't want to reintroduce one for the sake of spill prevention (see "Sippy Cup Syndrome" on page 59), consider bringing along (more reliable) or requesting (you're playing the odds) a few cups with lids and/or straws. Admittedly, the use of a straw isn't a foolproof method of avoiding spills (especially for children who have not yet learned to stop tipping while sipping), but nevertheless it will help you to keep your child's cup firmly grounded on her tray table instead of in her lap. It's also a good idea to ask the flight attendant to fill your child's cup only half full, and make sure that you take control of the can (and subsequent pouring) if she leaves it behind.

- **When Their Cups Runneth Over.** It makes no difference how old your children are or how long they have been out of diapers—if your child gets to drink on the airplane, a subsequent trip to the lavatory well in advance of anticipated descent should not, in our opinion, be optional.

## To Pee or Not to Pee

Be forewarned that airplane travel can pose problems for even those kids who have long-since proven their potty-training prowess. Being aware of the several factors working against having your child reach your destination dry may be reason enough for you to rethink your in-flight beverage service strategy.

- When faced with multiple offers to drink, children are usually more than willing to oblige.

- Young children's bladders can only hold a limited number of ounces—an estimated 1 ounce of liquid per year of age—and the time between when they feel the urge to go and when they *have* to go is often relatively short. Add these 2 realities together and it only makes sense that the younger the child, the shorter the time you have to ensure their safe and dry arrival to the lavatory.

- The added special effect of caffeine-containing drinks (ie, speeding up the need to pee) has a way of catching unsuspecting kids *and* parents unprepared to absorb the consequences.

- There are many characteristics of airplane travel that are guaranteed to be outside of your control—turbulence, a long line at the lavatory, and those times during both takeoff and landing when no degree of bladder distension warrants getting out of your seat. When faced with such delays, you may well find yourself with a problem on your hands and pee in your child's seat.

### Baby Beverages

- **Formula.** Formula is not negotiable, nor is it readily available during air travel. We therefore advise over-packing your supply by at least 3 times the amount you would ordinarily use. Be sure to consider how you plan to keep premixed formula cool, as well as allot time for warming, since the typical hot-water bottle bath can take what many babies consider to be intolerably long. While recent security regulations do *not* restrict the type or amount of infant formula you are able to carry on (so long as you actually have a baby along with you), it's well worth checking for any changes in carry-on rules before departure. You can find the Transportation Security Administration's guidelines at www.tsa.gov/travelers.

## Just Add Water

Instead of packing premixed bottles of formula, try putting the appropriate amount of premeasured powdered formula into each of your baby's bottles, secure the nipples and lids, and then toss them into your carry-on. The only thing left for you to do will be to add the corresponding amount of room-temperature water and mix. This pack-the-powder-only technique alleviates the need for refrigeration, bottle warming, customer service, and en route bottle washing—all of which can ultimately test a baby's patience and can be adapted to suit changing regulations: If increased airport security dictates a limit on the transport of water, it is fairly safe to assume that bottled water will be readily available once you've passed through security—either for purchase in the terminal or on the airplane. Don't be tempted to use water from the lavatory sinks, though, since studies have shown that it has the distinct possibility of being contaminated.

- **Breastfeeding.** From an availability standpoint, breastfeeding is a traveling mother's surefire solution to being well-prepared. That said, doing so in a 17-inch wide seat can sometimes be a bit challenging (especially for those who err on the side of modesty). If you choose to bring along bottles of pumped breast milk, you will want to take into account the same security restrictions and refrigeration requirements as apply to formula.

### Taking Matters Into Your Own Hands

The food that is served on most airlines these days counts as limited fare at best. Regardless of whether the time at which your family chooses to fly overlaps with what is clearly recognized as breakfast, lunch, or dinnertime the world over, your odds of being offered anything more than a bag of pretzels are still going to be slim. Even on the occasional flight that *does* provide a more substantial offering of food, you may need to come financially prepared, since all-inclusive flights seem to have become a thing of the very distant past. And knowing that a carefully timed 3-hour trip has the distinct potential to turn into a 10-hour misadventure, the last thing you want is to be caught empty-handed. The

🍜 In-Flight Nursing Know-How ☕

As we discussed in our book *Heading Home With Your Newborn: From Birth to Reality,* nursing an infant on an airplane presents its own unique set of challenges. Especially if your baby's car seat is in the window seat, you are in the middle seat, and a complete stranger is on the aisle encroaching on your shared armrest (which, as you know, is not just hypothetical), breastfeeding comfortably may seem like an oxymoron. Here are a few suggestions that can really help.

- **One-sided.** If the flight is short or you find yourself uncomfortably close to your seatmate, nursing on just one side while saving the other for when you get off the plane may be an acceptable option.

- **At an Angle.** Close quarters can greatly limit a breastfeeding mother's chance of privacy. Simply angling your body so that you're facing the window before trying to breastfeed can help minimize your degree of exposure.

- **Covering Up.** For the sake of modesty or convenience, bear in mind how much you want to bare, and wear a shirt you are particularly comfortable breastfeeding in, such as a loose-fitting top layer, a button-down blouse, or custom-designed breastfeeding attire.

- **Layering.** Use your jacket, a blanket, a magazine, or even your baby carrier or sling as a practical way of preventing your fellow passengers from having a bird's-eye view.

- **Stalling.** Nursing in the lavatory may seem like a reasonable last resort, but it generally poses a huge inconvenience for fellow passengers and isn't exactly hygienic. In other words, we don't recommend it.

reduced availability and variety of food on flights can come as quite a rude awakening for kids who are accustomed to having an abundance of choices, who are used to eating on demand or getting special fares, and who are particularly picky. If this is true of your child, be sure to prepare him (and yourself) accordingly. If your child is very young, has yet to master the concept of take-it-or-leave-it, and patience isn't yet a virtue he possesses, we suggest that you take mealtime matters into your own hands and equip yourself as follows.

- **Baby Food.** If you find feeding your baby pureed foods to be challenging on a good day, you certainly won't find it to be any easier in the confines of the cabin. In the few months after being introduced to baby foods, most babies won't miss it on travel days so long as they have plenty to drink along the way. And by the time babies are introduced to table foods (around 9 months or so), they can typically get by with makeshift meals and snacks in lieu of a jar of baby food. That said, unopened containers of baby food are practical to pack both because they do not require refrigeration and because you do not need to carry along any remains. Be sure to check current travel restrictions, however, since the 3-ounce limit on liquids, gels, and other less-than-solid substances has also been known to apply to baby food. Finally, remember to prepare for the accompanying mealtime mess by packing plenty of bibs, wipes, clothes, and diapers for what will almost certainly follow.

 **Three Ounces of Prevention**

Packing your carry-on with food and drink in anticipation of your child's in-transit needs (and wants) is a good idea, but one that has become significantly more challenging. With very few exceptions, the Transportation Security Administration (TSA) now requires that *all* liquids and/or gels—whether they serve as toiletries or sustenance—must be stored in 3-ounce (or smaller) containers that all fit into a single, quart-sized, zip-top, clear plastic bag for screening purposes. Unfortunately, most of the prepackaged snack items we know of exceed this 3-ounce limit (consider the 3.9-ounce Mott's applesauce container, 6-ounce Yoplait, or the 4.23-ounce mini Juicy Juice box, for example). Be aware that simply emptying out half of a 6-ounce container won't make the cut.

- **Snacks.** You don't need to go overboard, but stashing several finger foods and snacks can really come in handy. For the sake of convenience, avoid items that are sticky or require refrigeration, do any necessary slicing or dicing ahead of time, and put individual servings of each ready-to-serve snack in separate and easily accessible Baggies. Examples of relatively healthy foods that travel well include Cheerios, crackers, pretzels, pudding, applesauce, unpeeled bananas, sliced fruit, and carrot sticks (for older kids).

- **Meals.** Consider whether your travel coincides with one or more mealtimes, since snacks only last so long in satisfying some children's hunger. When planning your trip and booking your flights, be conservative in your estimate of how much time you'll need before and between flights to feed your family. Arriving too late to eat before boarding or finding oneself faced with unexpectedly short layovers are but a couple of prime reasons why we suggest packing some semblance of a meal just in case. Peanut butter sandwiches are perhaps the most commonly used, if for no other reason than they don't need to be refrigerated. Just take extra caution to consider the potential for food allergies—including those of the passengers seated around you.

 Peanuts on a Plane

If you have a child with known (or even suspected) peanut allergies and don't want to experience peanut problems at 30,000 feet, it's important to plan ahead. With the increase in peanut allergies (see "Allergies and Intolerances" on page 197), several airlines have stopped handing out packages of peanuts or mixed nuts as their snack of choice. When we last checked, those leading the peanut-free airways included American, United, Northwest, Jet Blue, Spirit, AirTran, US Airways, America West, and ATA. Other airlines may provide peanut "buffer zones" (no peanuts within 3 rows of an allergic passenger, for example) or remove peanuts from certain flights upon advance request. Because airline policies change frequently, be sure to ask your ticketing agent if you are interested in these accommodations. Remember to also take matters into your own hands by checking the seats for any stray peanuts that may have been left behind, bring "safe" back-up foods for the flight, and pack your clearly labeled emergency medications along with written instructions from your doctor regarding their proper use.

PART VI

# just for the health of it

CHAPTER 28

# keeping up with the curves

**Are you afraid your child is becoming too fat?** Do your relatives insist she's looking too thin? Have you let her quirky eating demands go too far or do you think they are of no real consequence? In any weighty discussions involving diet and nutrition, it can be quite difficult to maintain one's objectivity. Especially when the day-to-day food fights are wearing you down, we suggest you take a look past your child, her habits, and what is (or isn't) making it past her mouth and make use of her growth charts as a reliable measure of whether you and your child are on the right track or headed toward trouble. Since weight gain—too much, too little, or just right—can be affected by a child's eating habits, following your child's growth over time will provide you with a healthy perspective on how your nutritional efforts are shaping up.

## To Each His Own

No matter how much or how little they eat, some kids are destined to be big; others will always be relatively small. But regardless of size, just about all healthy kids follow a very predictable pattern of growth. From the first day you set foot in your pediatrician's office, you can rest assured that he or she will be regularly plotting (the charts) on your child's behalf. As each of your child's height and weight measurements (and head size, up until the age of 3) gets added to his graph and the resulting dots are connected, you will end up with your child's very own growth curve.

Defining Features of the  Growth Charts

For the past 3 decades, the Centers for Disease Control and Prevention's growth charts have served as the gold standard for evaluating the growth of children from birth through 20 years. Most recently updated in 2000, these charts are based on measurements of height, weight, and head size taken from thousands of North American children. Although they are commonly used to graphically illustrate the typical growth patterns for boys and girls, it is important to note that they do not accurately reflect the expected growth of *all* children. This is especially true for children of diverse ethnic and cultural backgrounds, those born with particular medical conditions, and babies who are exclusively breastfed. For children with Down syndrome, those born prematurely, and those who are exclusively breastfed, special growth charts are available.

## Getting to the Points

While growth curves are much easier to understand and best explained in person, we wanted to toss in a few practical points of our own to help you navigate your way around the curves and more effectively read between the lines.

### It's All Relative: BMI

Weight is not nearly as useful as a stand-alone measurement as it is when height is factored into the equation. Relatively new on the scene, body mass index (or BMI) is a number that takes into account weight relative to height. It is now considered to be the best reflection of body fat and, therefore, a very good indicator of whether any child older than 2 years is overweight, underweight, or has comfortably settled somewhere in between. BMI calculations help put an end once and for all to the classic rationalization, "I'm not overweight, I'm just undertall!"

Unlike for adults, whose BMI goals remain the same even as they get older, it's useful to keep in mind that the ideal BMI numbers for children vary according to both age and gender.

### Figuring Out BMI

$$BMI = \frac{(Weight/Height^*)}{Height} \times 703$$

For example, let's say you have a 5-year-old girl. She weighs 40 pounds and is 3 feet 7 inches (43 inches) tall. 40 divided by 43 = 0.93; 0.93 divided by 43 = 0.02; all you have to do is multiply by 703 to calculate the BMI, which equals 15.2. As you can see on the chart below, this example daughter's BMI is right at 50% for age.

*Where weight is measured in pounds and height is in inches.

### *Maintain a Healthy Distance*

Want to know how we routinely suggest to parents that they should look at any growth curve? From at least an arm's length away. Since all children have their up and down days (or weeks) when it comes to both what they eat and what they weigh, simply taking a big step back will help prevent you from focusing too closely on any single measurement—especially one that mistakenly happens to fall off the beaten path.

## Not All Points Are Created Equal

There are plenty of reasons why a point or two on the growth curves may go astray without being a cause for concern. They include:

- **On a Different Scale.** Using a different scale from one measurement to the next can yield very different results.
- **When You've Gotta Go.** Whether your child goes (to the bathroom, that is) just before or just after being weighed can tip the scales one way or the other. The resulting effect on weight is usually most noticeable for babies, since slight variations are more obvious the less children weigh to begin with.
- **Padding the Numbers.** We know the doctor's office can be a bit chilly, but anything short of full disclosure (keeping the clothes, shoes, or diapers on) can add extra ounces, if not pounds.
- **Sick of It.** Recent illnesses can easily skew a child's weight measurements, since children often lose their appetites when they're sick. Fortunately, children are good at gaining right back whatever they have lost once they return to being healthy (see "Feeding Through Sick and Slim" on page 189).
- **A Moving Target.** Weight is not the only measurement that leaves room for error. Even length or height readings can be quite distorted depending on how cooperative a young child feels about being stretched out or standing tall.

### *Average Isn't All It Plots Out to Be*

It's only natural to want your child to be normal and fit in, but don't make the mistake of presuming that the middle of the road is where your child should be when it comes to her growth curves. What really counts is *not* your child's proximity to the 50th percentile, but that she is keeping pace.

### *Bigger Isn't Always Better*

It can also be tempting for parents to equate their children's higher percentile results with a job well done (and conversely, interpret low-ranking percentiles as a poor performance). But unless your child's weight *and* height measurements match up, bigger does *not* mean better. Unlike test scores or the results of a race, your child's progress up the growth curve is not a competition to be won or lost, and there's definitely no prize for finishing first.

### *Staying in Your Lane*

Be on the lookout for any crossing of curves. Whenever a child's individual growth curve starts to take a conspicuous detour—deviating either upward or downward enough to cross into a neighboring lane or two—it is reason to pay closer attention. If nothing else, this warrants more frequent weigh-ins at the doctor's office to see if the trend continues. If necessary, take a closer look at what's responsible for the change in course.

---

### 🥣 Food Is Not the Only Driving Force ☕

If your child's weight gain starts to fall short or overshoot what is expected of him, it's entirely possible that poor eating habits are to blame. That said, keep in mind that food intake or the lack thereof is not the *only* potential cause for crossing curves. When growth heads off-track to the point of concern, take comfort in knowing that your pediatrician can be particularly helpful in determining if there are other contributing factors.

---

### Mealtime Milestones: Shifting Gears on Growth

When left unprepared for what lies ahead, parents can easily be thrown for a loop by those predictable twists and turns that may show up as changes in both their child's day-to-day eating habits and their growth curves.

- **First Year: Expect Steep Curves.** Babies grow faster during their first year of life than they hopefully ever will again—typically doubling their birth weight by the time they reach a mere 4 months of age and tripling it by their first birthdays. This early rapid rate of growth understandably calls for both a hearty appetite and a steep rise to the growth curves. Some babies who are born small may even try to make up for lost time and catch up to a higher curve than the one they were born on.

- **9 to 15 Months: Warning—Reduced Speed Ahead.** Somewhere between the ages of 9 and 15 months, it is normal for toddlers (especially those who have been exclusively breastfed) to slow down the pace a bit. After months of yielding to the hefty nutritional demands of their babies' first year, parents who have not surveyed what lies ahead on the curves can be caught off guard by both their children's decreased appetites and the posting of lower-than-expected weight gains.

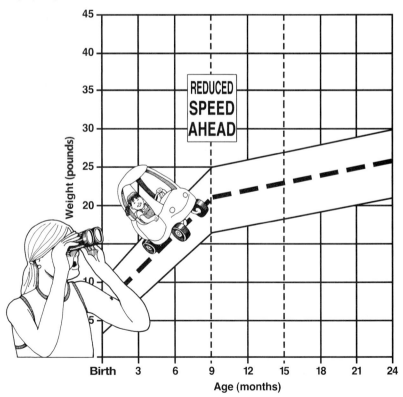

- **1+ Years: Cruise Control.** Now is the time when your child will likely have mapped out her course and defined which growth curve (percentile) she intends to follow for the next several years. Her growth should now be much more slow and steady—allowing, of course, for the occasional bump in the road caused by such factors as picky eating, routine illness, or even mismeasurement.

- **2 Years: Expanding Your Horizons.** Your child can now graduate to a new growth chart—one that will be able to pick up seamlessly where her previous curves left off and allow you to track her growth from 2 to 20 years. This is the age at which your child's height will be taken standing up, her weight will be 4 times what it was at birth, and BMI measurements will be the best marker of whether your child is becoming either underweight or overweight.

- **3+ Years: Going Nowhere.** If you're now considering the possibility that your ultra-picky preschooler is terribly underweight, you'll likely be reassured by the fact that growth should remain comparatively slow for the next several years—a concept you can easily confirm by taking a quick look at the relatively flat portion of the growth curves that characterizes this age.

 Measuring Up

Some quick and easy methods of measuring up include:

- Children double, triple, and quadruple their birth weight at predictable times.

| Weight (relative to birth weight) | Age |
| --- | --- |
| 2x | 4–6 months |
| 3x | 1 year |
| 4x | 2 years |

- Kids 2 and older gain about 5 pounds a year.
- You can also estimate how tall your child will be as an adult by doubling his height at 2 years.

**Keeping Your Own Curves in Check**

It's not coincidental that overweight parents tend to have overweight children, so getting your own weight into a healthy range is a good first step. Now that you have a better understanding of where your child has been and where you want her to head, we hope you'll take a moment to reflect on some curves of your own. In the spirit of setting a good example, you can start by figuring out what your own BMI is. Remember, BMIs are not set in stone, so if yours isn't where you would like it to be, adjusting your own eating habits and activity level accordingly will inevitably benefit both you *and* your child.

CHAPTER 29

# a vitamin a day

**Do you ever glance despairingly** at what goes untouched on your toddler's plate or consider what never makes it there in the first place and wish you could buy yourself a nutritional safety net to go along with a good book on the subject of food fights? If so, you are not alone. It has been estimated that just over half of all preschoolers are given multivitamins. We're pretty sure that's a good bit more than are served broccoli on any given day. And we're quite sure we can relate to the reasons why. When the going gets tough, it is often a whole lot easier to reach for a quick fix in a bottle of Flintstones vitamins and forget the fight. The fact that there are so many parents who do just that isn't so much a food fight, per se, but a reflection on the parental feelings so many of us share that what we're feeding our children is nutritionally inadequate. While we can definitely understand the sentiment, it compels us to address the fundamental question: What role should multivitamins play in your child's diet, and is it you or your child that stands to benefit from them more?

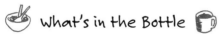 What's in the Bottle

The name "multivitamin" can be a bit deceiving, since most bottles of multi-vitamins contain not just some combination of the 13 essential vitamins, but also dietary minerals such as zinc and iron.

### Who Needs 'Em, Anyway?

We'll come right out and say what most nutrition experts have been saying all along: Most children don't *need* vitamin supplements at all!

Yes, we realize that the perfect, vegetable-loving, cooperative eater we all long for doesn't exist. But even taking all food fights into consideration, there are nevertheless very few instances in which a child's diet is likely to leave him truly deficient. If you need further convincing, we suggest you consider the following facts:

- The amount your child needs to eat to get enough vitamins and minerals from his food alone is probably much smaller than you think.

- Even for the pickiest of eaters, it doesn't take more than a very few picks from each of the basic food groups for children to get their recommended daily dose.

- Many vitamins can be stored in the body. This means that your child doesn't have to eat each and every one, every day—affording you the option of spreading your efforts at achieving a balanced diet out over the course of a week or two without spreading the vitamins too thin.

- Ironically enough, parents who are most likely to give multivitamins are also those who are most likely to be feeding their children healthy diets in the first place.

- Vitamins can be found in some unlikely sources. Calcium doesn't just have to come from cows, since it is contained in both supplements and many nondairy foods ranging from salmon, tofu, spinach, and sardines to rhubarb, baked beans, bok choy, and almonds—admittedly not all of which are an easy sell at the dinnertable, but at least you have plenty to choose from!

- And finally, many foods these days are fortified. That means that even if your child favors foods that do not come naturally loaded with all of the necessary nutrients, all hope is not lost; it's entirely possible that food manufacturers have added them in for you. Classic examples include the vitamin D fortification of milk, margarine, and pudding, and the calcium contained in kid-friendly foods such as orange juice, cereals, breads, and even Eggo waffles.

### When Multivitamins Are a Must

There are a few well-recognized times when children actually do need supplemental vitamins. They include:

- **Breastfeeding *D*-mands.** Babies who are primarily breastfed should be given vitamin D supplements starting no later than 2 months of age to compensate for the fact that it does not pass through breast milk well, leaving breastfed babies with short supply. Vitamin D is important for bones, and too little of it can cause a condition called rickets.

- **Iron Implications.** A baby's stored-up iron supply normally drops to a low point by 9 to 12 months. Most babies can get by just fine with the iron they get from their food, primarily baby cereal and formula, and routine screening can easily identify those in need of a little extra iron in the form of supplemental drops until their diets can go it alone.

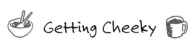

### Getting Cheeky

If you find yourself in the position of trying to get your baby or toddler to swallow any type of vitamin drops, we suggest you tuck the medicine dropper into the corner of her mouth (between her gums or teeth and her cheek) instead of aiming for the middle of her mouth. This practical method of medication administration minimizes your chances that what you squirt in is going to be spit out.

- **Fluoride Fill-ins.** Fluoride supplements may be recommended for infants 6 months and up and children who do not have the benefit of fluoride in their drinking water. Fluoride is also absent from pre-mixed formula and breast milk (see "Brushing Up" on page 127).

- **Vegetarian Variations.** Any child raised on a vegetarian diet requires special consideration when it comes to getting all of the recommended vitamins and minerals, since certain nutrients such as vitamin B12, vitamin D, iron, and zinc are found mainly in animal products. Iron-deficiency anemia is a particularly common problem when meat is missing from a child's diet.

### What Do Vitamins Buy *You?*

With the overwhelming amount of evidence and expert advice suggesting that we could, in good conscience, cross multivitamins off our shopping lists altogether, we feel the need to redirect the discussion and ask why they continue to be a staple food substitute in households across America. The way we see it, multivitamins' popularity isn't just based on what they do for kids (or the fact that they often taste like candy), but what they do for parents. We have come to the conclusion that parents who give their children multivitamins are potentially buying *themselves* 3 fundamental things.

1. **Time.** As in the time it takes to outlast the predictable picky practices and dietary deviations so common (and so frustrating) in the early years of eating. Vitamin supplements can reasonably be used as a temporizing measure to fill in any real or perceived nutritional gaps in your child's diet while affording you the time to overcome any of the underlying dietary challenges you have found yourself faced with.

2. **Peace of Mind.** Multivitamins serve the purpose of giving parents additional peace of mind—allowing them to sleep at night knowing that they've got all the bases of the food pyramid covered. This, in turn, takes the pressure off of mealtime and makes it more likely to be fun—2 very important strategies for feeding success.

3. **An Excuse.** While buying yourself some time and peace of mind is unquestionably valuable and should not be discounted, using a multivitamin as an excuse to drop your ongoing efforts to teach your child lifelong healthy eating habits is, to be blunt, a poor one at best. While multivitamins admittedly can help to avert battles, fill voids, and serve as a harmless dietary Band-Aid when given as directed, they should not be used long term to cover up a lousy diet.

### Food or Drug Administration?

When all is said and done, we know full well that multivitamins are here to stay. We therefore want to leave those of you who plan to make use of them with one last thought. According to the US Food and Drug Administration, vitamins are technically considered food. That said, for the sake of safety you are far better off convincing your child that multivitamins are medicine, since large doses (most notably of vitamins A and D, zinc, and iron) have the real potential to cause harm. The fact that vitamin supplements are readily available in tantalizing flavors and masquerade in kid-friendly forms—everything from gummi bears to cartoon characters—definitely makes them go down easier…so easy, in fact, that your child is liable to crave them. It is therefore particularly prudent for parents to make the distinction early and often so that children learn to take their vitamins as seriously as they would any other medicine. Be sure to restrict access by keeping multivitamins (not to mention all other pills and medications) safely out of your child's reach, buying and keeping them in child-resistant containers, and making a point of overseeing their daily administration. Finally, whatever you do, don't call them candy.

CHAPTER 30

# feeding through sick and slim

### Feed a Fever, Starve a Cold?

Whether it's "feed a fever, starve a cold" or vice versa, we'll be honest with you—we don't think this phrase (reportedly dating back to the mid-1500s) has much mealtime merit. Feeding a child with a fever *or* a cold is generally easier said than done, and starving a cold is often not a matter of choice but rather a statement of fact. Regardless of whether they have vomiting, diarrhea, stuffy noses, or coughs, kids who are virally afflicted almost always lose their appetites, and getting them to

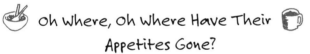 Oh Where, Oh Where Have Their Appetites Gone?

- **1 to 2 Days *Before* Illness: Without a Trace.** Well before fever rears its ugly head or vomiting and diarrhea burst onto the scene, children may lose their appetites for no apparent reason and parents are left scratching their heads, wondering where it might have gone.

- **Days 1 to 3: Clued In.** Appetite is still lost, but now other symptoms appear and parents are tipped off as to what they're dealing with. Some of the first symptoms to show up are fever and vomiting, which share a particular knack for throwing a child's appetite out of whack.

- **Days 2 to 14: Counting the Days.** It is understandably hard for parents to come to terms with the fact that the common cold can easily last 2 weeks. It is even more disconcerting to discover that one's appetite can remain at bay even longer. Long after the last cough or sniffle has subsided and the Tylenol and tissues have been tucked away, it may still take an additional week or so before a child's appetite is restored to its rightful owner.

> ### 🥢 Classic Comfort Food: ☕ Chicken Noodle Soup
>
> You can take comfort in knowing that the most classic of all comfort foods dished out during times of illness is not only good, but may actually be good for you. Scientists who tested this generations-old culinary remedy reportedly found that chicken noodle soup helped to both reduce inflammation and decrease congestion. If you're wondering whether anything could possibly compare to the kind your grandmother made, for what it's worth, researchers at the University of Nebraska apparently also found that canned chicken noodle soup was as effective as soup made from scratch.

## Symptom-Specific Strategies

There are several specific illness-related symptoms that stand to throw a wrench in your child's eating routine. Here is a closer look at several of the more common ones and some advice on how to best handle them. If your home remedies prove unsuccessful, or if you are concerned that your child seems extremely sick, put down the book and pick up the phone or visit your pediatrician.

### *Snotty Noses: Getting Mucus to Make Way*

An excess of mucus may, at first glance, seem relatively trivial in the spectrum of symptoms your child is sure to come down with over the years. That said, snot has the distinct ability to interfere with a child's eating habits both from the unsettling standpoint of where it comes to rest and because it blocks airflow. Nobody likes things stuck in their mouths when their noses are stuffed. This principle applies especially to babies, who have the narrowest nostrils and tend to be the least tolerant of a plugged nose when trying to eat or drink. The fact that one's nose is connected to the back of one's throat doesn't help matters either, since a nose filled with mucus inevitably leads to a throat and/or stomach filled with a lot of the same. Not fun, certainly not appetizing, and sometimes enough to stir up trouble and cause gagging and/or vomiting.

In hopes of increasing the odds that your stuffy-nosed child will be willing and able to keep on eating—or at least drinking—we recommend trying out the following methods:

- **Wait.** Don't be too quick to offer food or drink immediately after your child wakes up, since children tend to be the most congested after they've been lying down and sleeping. Give any accumulated mucus a chance to clear itself out before trying to get anything in.

- **Elevate.** Both while sleeping and while awake, elevating your child's head a bit can help the drainage situation. For infants, this generally means elevating the head of the crib during sleep and putting them in an incline seat or holding them upright when awake.

- **Moisturize.** Running a cool mist vaporizer or humidifier nearby but well out of your child's reach can help to loosen things up a bit, as can sitting with your child in a steamy bathroom or having her take a shower, once she's old enough to do so safely.

- **Remove.** While you can feel free to use a bulb suction along with some saline nose drops to take the matter into your own hands and clear the way, just keep in mind that this technique, while effective, isn't exactly comfortable and you probably won't get away with using it for too long before your baby protests.

 **Mucus Milestone: All Stuffed Up**
**and No Way to Blow**

Most children can't blow their noses effectively until at least the age of 2 or 3. The younger your child is, the less likely he is to be able to move mucus out of the way and let the air flow in (and out), and the more likely he is to be irritated by your well-intentioned assaults on his nose and dignity.

### *Vomiting: Getting Things to Settle Down*

Vomiting is not fun. It's even less so when your child does it, since it generally leaves you with your hands (and sometimes your lap) full and your child miserable. Getting a child with a vomiting illness to keep anything down can be a formidable challenge. There are, however, a few tricks of the parenting trade that can help you in this regard.

- **Take It Slow and Steady.** Think of it this way: An unsettled stomach is highly likely to strike out against food and/or drink, and your mission is to sneak them in without causing an uprising. The best way to do this is to give small amounts more frequently—offering a teaspoon or two every 5 to 10 minutes for example. If your child is so thirsty that she has no intention of slowing down, be creative. Try offering her Popsicles or Jell-O, or let her drink from a spoon—all methods meant to appease her but which will slow her down nonetheless.

- **Allow Time to Settle.** It's only natural that parents' immediate reaction to vomiting is to want to replace all that has been lost without delay. Given that a child who has just finished vomiting is very likely to have a stomach just waiting for a reason to vomit again, consider holding off for a little while (at least a half an hour or so) to let things settle before tempting fate.

- **Be on Red Alert.** As a point of practicality and carpet preservation, we also advise avoiding foods and drinks that are red when your child's chances of vomiting are high, since they can both stain the decor and on occasion may be mistaken for blood.

### Diarrhea: Problems With Rapid Transit

For the most part, you can approach feeding a child with diarrhea by using the same techniques described above. A few additional diarrhea-specific suggestions include:

- **Limit Restrictions.** Children with diarrhea may regain their appetite well before all of their intestinal issues are resolved. Although eating and drinking before the diarrhea has disappeared completely may trigger a swift response from a recovering child's digestive tract, it is usually temporary, does not require any restriction of food or fluids, and is rarely a cause for concern.

## Replacing Losses

Diarrhea can rob children both of their appetites and of important mineral-containing fluids. Fortunately, there are special drinks designed specifically to help parents replace the water and salt that are inevitably lost in the process. These so-called replacement fluids can be extremely helpful in managing everything from moderate to moderately severe diarrhea. Furthermore, they come not only in bottles, but in the more desirable form of freezer pops as well. These widely available products are offered in a variety of flavors and can be found in nearly every grocery store or pharmacy. They include:

- Pedialyte
- Infalyte
- ReVital
- LiquiLytes

Custom-designed for use in young children with diarrhea, there is certainly no harm in reaching for these electrolyte solutions to treat your vomiting child as well, as long as you make sure to contact your pediatrician if your child's symptoms require the use of these solutions for more than a day or so. Sports drinks such as Gatorade can be useful but are high in sugar and are not as well tailored to replace salt losses as are the pediatric electrolyte solutions.

- **Anticipate End Results.** Don't be alarmed if and when diarrhea causes food to move through the intestinal tract much more quickly than usual. The end result of rapid transit is that any food that children put in their mouths stands a good chance of escaping relatively unscathed and undigested out the other end.

- **Let Food Work in Your Favor.** When it comes to diarrhea, certain foods are felt to help by bulking things up and therefore slowing things down. Best known is the BRAT diet, consisting of *b*ananas, *r*ice, *a*pples (or *a*pplesauce), and *t*oast (or sometimes *t*ea). While it doesn't hurt to offer your child these foods, they tend to be lower in calories and protein than a regular diet. It is for this reason that the BRAT diet is no longer recommended as the sole solution to diarrhea. Instead, it is best to offer your child her usual diet and plenty of fluids while avoiding high-fat and high-sugar foods—a good idea in both times of sickness *and* in health. If it's a slower pace you're hoping for, more common symptoms that may clue you in to a potential allergy *or* intolerance include:

- A whole host of intestinal symptoms. Nausea, stomachaches, spitting up or vomiting, diarrhea, and blood in the stools can all occur after eating an offending food.

- Rashes. Food reactions may come in the form of a contact rash (usually around the mouth), hives (more specific to allergies than intolerances and scattered anywhere across the body), and the development or worsening of eczema.

- More severe symptoms—difficulty breathing, difficulty swallowing, wheezing, and/or swelling (especially of the eyes, lips, tongue, face, and/or throat)—are all much more suggestive of a true allergic reaction requiring immediate medical attention.

 An Adrenaline Rush

Adrenaline, also called *epinephrine,* is the best medication available to counteract a severe allergic reaction. It comes in an easy-to-inject form most commonly known as either an EpiPen or TwinJect. In one research study, only a third of parents of children with an identified peanut allergy owned and knew how to use this lifesaving medicine. With that in mind, we strongly suggest that if your child has a severe allergy of any type, be sure to discuss the use of one of these injectors with your child's doctor. If it is deemed necessary, be sure to get not only yourself but any of your child's caregivers a prescription for one, fill it, and learn how to store it and use it properly. For your best shot at combating a serious reaction, make sure your child never leaves home without it.

### Mealtime Milestones: Making Timely Introductions

Adopting a degree of defensive eating as part of your overall nutritional game plan can go a long way toward reducing your child's risk. Although food allergies and intolerances can occur at any age, most show up during a child's first year. Many of the simple measures routinely employed in children's earliest feeding routines are based on straightforward principles of allergy prevention, giving us the ability to bypass some food allergy confrontations entirely and pinpoint others before they become a problem. The following are some of the most common for each age group.

- **Before Birth.** Although studies have shown that infants develop a preference for flavors they were exposed to before birth, there is no definitive evidence that restricting a mother's diet during pregnancy reduces her child's future risk of food allergies. Given these findings, along with the knowledge that some of the more allergenic foods are felt to be nutritious and beneficial for both mom and the growing infant, eliminating these foods during pregnancy is not generally deemed necessary. That said, some experts err on the side of caution and advocate for abstinence from the more allergenic foods for those with a strong family history.

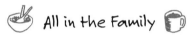

### All in the Family

Having a family history of food allergies basically means that at least one of your family members has already been found to be food-allergic, and is important to take into consideration because allergies, in general, tend to run in families. Although you can't predict which type of allergies a child is going to get, a child with 2 parents who both have allergies has a 75% likelihood of also developing one. If allergies only run on one side of the family, a child's risk drops to approximately 35%. This is in contrast to those children who have no family history at all; while not completely immune to the problem, they only stand a 15% chance of being diagnosed.

- **Birth to 4 Months.** The fact that your baby will be feasting on an exclusive diet of breast milk and/or formula in his first several months means that your chance of being confronted with food allergies or intolerances is primarily limited to milk or soy allergies and milk-soy protein intolerance (MSPI)—a condition that occurs in only approximately 5% of infants. If your baby happens to develop any of the signs of MSPI, such as gassiness, abdominal pain, vomiting, diarrhea, poor weight gain, and/or bloody stools, be sure to have your pediatrician further assess the situation, test your baby's poop, and help make the diagnosis. Given that as many as half of babies who have difficulty digesting cow's milk protein (as found in basic baby formulas) also have problems processing soy, the solution to the problem of MSPI generally comes in the form of a pediatrician-recommended hypoallergenic (elemental) formula.

For breastfed babies, the jury is still out. While it is not well established that changing a breastfeeding mother's diet is necessary, most pediatricians have found that doing so can make a noticeable difference in some babies' dispositions. You can certainly use some trial and error to determine if certain components of your diet seem to cause trouble, just don't drive yourself crazy and go to dietary extremes all in the name of a fussy baby (see "The Price of Gas" on page 215).

- **4 to 6 Months.** Waiting until 4 to 6 months of age to start introducing your baby to solids is the easiest and most commonly recommended way to avoid both present and future allergies. Especially if your baby is still satisfied with exclusively breastfeeding, it is considered beneficial to hold off on solids until 6 months. Remember that the types of food you want to introduce first are those that you'll see listed as Stage 1 (see At This Stage of the Game on page 27).

## 🍜 🍴 Taking It One Day at a Time ☕

Some experts suggest waiting a day or two between the introduction of each new food, while others recommend waiting a full 5. Whether you choose to wait 1 or 5 days or anywhere in between, the basic underlying principle remains the same: If a child happens to develop any signs or symptoms of a food allergy or intolerance, it makes life a whole lot easier if you're able to pick apart just which food was to blame. Although it is true that a good many food-related reactions occur within minutes to hours, some can take a full 2 days to make themselves known.

- **8 to 10 Months.** The foods you should choose to introduce to your 8- to 10-month-old will depend upon whether your baby has previously shown any signs of allergy problems and whether you and your pediatrician believe those nasty allergens are worth avoiding. At this age, most children's digestive systems can handle some processed dairy products such as yogurt or cheese. That said, regular cow's milk is not yet recommended, so be sure to stick with breast milk or infant formula. Unless you have a specific reason to be on the lookout for allergens, this is also the age when it is acceptable to introduce wheat-containing bread products and pastas. Although berries and citrus have a bad reputation in regard to allergy, they are actually unlikely to cause genuine allergy symptoms. They *have*, however, been known to irritate the skin and digestive tract enough to result in rashes, diarrhea, or excess gas—all reasons enough for many parents to hold off on introducing them for a while.

- **1 Year and Up.** By the time they reach their first birthdays, most babies can switch to regular cow's milk without a problem. And assuming your family is not at increased risk for food allergies, you are also likely to get the go-ahead from your pediatrician to introduce just about anything and everything in the way of table foods, as long as they don't pose a choking risk (see "All Choking Aside" on page 229).

### Better Late or Never

Timing may not be everything, but in the case of food allergies in children who may be especially prone, it may be best to adjust your timeline. In hopes of preventing the development of food allergies, some experts recommend that if an infant's parents, or one parent and a sibling, have allergies, then it is wise to wait until age 1 before offering dairy, age 2 for eggs, and age 3 for peanuts, nuts, fish, and shellfish. While this delay is commonly recommended, it's worth bearing in mind that its effectiveness has not been proven. On the other hand, if your infant already shows allergic problems, it may be appropriate to hold off on some of the more allergenic foods until your doctor feels it is safe or runs some tests. When all is said and done, just remember that you always have the option of leaving the more high-risk foods off the menu.

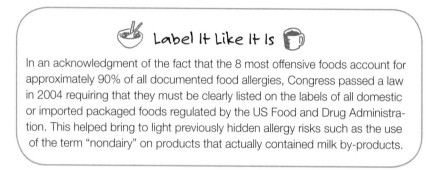

## Label It Like It Is

In an acknowledgment of the fact that the 8 most offensive foods account for approximately 90% of all documented food allergies, Congress passed a law in 2004 requiring that they must be clearly listed on the labels of all domestic or imported packaged foods regulated by the US Food and Drug Administration. This helped bring to light previously hidden allergy risks such as the use of the term "nondairy" on products that actually contained milk by-products.

### The Exceptional 8

Sure, practically every food has been implicated in triggering allergies in certain people, but you can effectively focus your efforts by zeroing in on those foods that are most likely to cause a commotion. The 8 biggest offenders have been clearly identified as milk, eggs, peanuts, tree nuts, fish, shellfish, wheat, and soy.

### 1. Much Ado About Milk

Cow's milk is not recommended for infants before a year of age for good reason. Not only does it run the risk of causing symptoms of unrest, but it may even trigger a true allergy to milk that might otherwise be avoided. Fortunately, less than 3% of children develop a true milk allergy in the first place, with half outgrowing this condition by age 1 year and 85% outgrowing it by age 4 to 6.

## Lactose Intolerance

For anyone without enough of the enzyme responsible for digesting lactose (called *lactase*), consuming large amounts of *any* dairy product can result in symptoms similar to a true milk allergy as well as cause bloating, cramping, nausea, diarrhea, and gas. Fortunately, children tend to have more lactase than adults, and even those children who are somewhat lactose-intolerant can handle small amounts of dairy at a time without difficulty. For anyone unable to go it alone, the dairy industry has conveniently found a way to include the missing enzyme in various milk products such as Lactaid.

Parents of children with true milk allergies should avoid serving just about all dairy products, and be wary of foods that contain milk and milk products—including cakes, breads, and even milk chocolate. While pasteurized goat's milk is sometimes recommended as a reasonable alternative, parents and pediatricians alike need to be aware that it, too, is likely to cause an allergic reaction, as well as lead to folic acid and iron deficiencies.

2. **Eggs-tra, Eggs-tra, Read All About 'Em**

   Approximately 1 out of every 20 children with allergies is allergic to eggs. Although both egg yolks and egg whites contain protein, it is the white part that is far more likely to cause allergic reactions. Some children with egg allergies may be OK eating the yolks or those foods that have a little egg baked in them such as bread, pasta, pancakes, and waffles. Still, keep an eye out and discuss your egg approach with your pediatrician because it's possible to have reactions to even small exposures.

## Eggs and Vaccines

Certain vaccines are made in eggs, and therefore run the risk of containing traces of egg protein. If your child has been diagnosed with an egg allergy, you should be sure to consult with your pediatrician about how to keep your child both safe and well-vaccinated.

- Both influenza and yellow fever vaccines are made in eggs. Given that children with egg allergies often have other conditions as well (such as asthma) that make them more at risk from the flu, special protocols have been put in place that may allow children who are allergic to eggs to still get the influenza vaccine in small doses and under close supervision.

- The measles-mumps-rubella (MMR) vaccine is made in chick embryo cells, not in eggs themselves. The amount of egg protein it therefore contains is at least 500 times less than that in the influenza vaccine, and several studies have now documented its safe use even in children with severe egg allergies.

- Despite its name, the *chicken*pox (varicella) vaccine does *not*, in fact, contain any egg and therefore poses no additional risk for those who are allergic to eggs.

### 3. Soy Story

OK, so tofu, tempeh, and tamari may never top your shopping lists, but we're willing to wager that some of your pantries are probably stocked with several other common sources of soy including soy sauce, canned tuna, and certain cereals, soups, and baked goods. Soy (short for soybeans) belongs to the legume family. Other members of this family include navy beans, kidney beans, string (as in green) beans, black beans, pinto beans, chickpeas (aka garbanzo beans), lentils, carob, and…you might not have guessed it—peanuts. As one of the least allergenic of the top 8, perhaps the most important moral of the soy story is that there is a close enough relationship between soy and peanuts that anyone deemed allergic to one should proceed with caution around the other.

### 4. The Problem With Peanuts

Although peanuts are by no means the most common cause of food allergies, the number of children with peanut allergies has doubled in recent years—translating to an estimated 1 out of every 125 children. And of all the foods that trigger allergies, none are better at it than peanuts since simply ingesting tiny amounts of peanuts can trigger severe allergic reactions. Add to that the fact that peanut butter still prevails in households, child care centers, and schools across America and peanuts still make their way into everything from sugar cookies, chocolate bars, and a good many cereals to the confines of airplane cabins (see "Plane and Simple: In-Flight Food Fights" on page 165) and it is easy to see why peanut allergies remain particularly problematic.

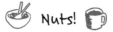 Nuts!

Food is not the only potential source of trouble for children with nut allergies. Cosmetics, lotions, and shampoos sometimes contain tree nut extracts, and everything from hacky sacks to pet food and bird seed run the risk of containing peanuts and/or tree nuts.

**5. Sometimes You Feel Like a Tree Nut**

If you're like us, your first reaction to the phrase "tree nut" may have been to wonder if you'd know one if it fell off a tree and hit you in the head. While food labels warning consumers about the presence of tree nuts are required to list them, we figured it would be helpful to list for you this fairly all-encompassing category, since tree nuts include everything from cashews, pecans, hazel nuts, Brazil nuts, macadamia nuts, and pistachios to hickory nuts, almonds, and walnuts. In a nutshell, these include just about every type of nut you can think of besides peanuts—and, of course, do*nuts*. While tree nuts are known to cause an allergic reaction all their own, as many as half of children with this type of allergy may also be at risk for a peanut allergy as well. For the purpose of safety-proofing the diet of nut-allergic children, many allergists therefore advise avoiding both peanuts and tree nuts altogether.

**6. Why Worry About Wheat?**

Wheat allergies, like soy, are less common than many of the other elite 8. As an easy precautionary measure, however, it makes sense for parents to steer clear of the wheat-containing baby cereals (which typically come packaged as either wheat or as mixed grain) until

### Gluten for Punishment

Collectively called gluten, the proteins in wheat, barley, and rye are known to be some of the most complex and difficult types of proteins to digest. Children can develop an intolerance for gluten that, in some cases, causes enough irritation of the intestinal lining to interfere with nutrient absorption. This can result in weight loss, diarrhea, anemia, and poor growth—all symptoms of a condition called *gluten-sensitive enteropathy* (also known as *celiac disease* or *celiac sprue*). Gluten sensitivity can develop at any age once gluten has been introduced into a child's diet, but it most commonly starts around the age of 2. No matter when it declares itself, a gluten-free diet is definitely not to be undertaken lightly, as it requires parents to seek the help of medical professionals and involves *significantly* altering what children eat.

babies reach at least 9 months of age. Once your baby is exposed to wheat in her diet—either in her baby cereal or in any of the many other wheat-containing foods such as breads, cookies, cakes, crackers, cereals, and pasta—it's worth watching for the characteristic signs of allergy or intolerance.

**7. Keeping Fish Out of the Fray**

Although neither of us made a habit of serving our children fish in their first year or two, some parents definitely do. This combined with the fact that reactions to fish are often severe and don't typically go away over time make it well worth mentioning. Interestingly, while many children allergic to one type of finned fish are allergic to most others, there are also those who are only allergic to certain fish; while salmon may cause trouble, they have no need to throw back the cod.

**8. Shunning Shellfish**

Shellfish include shrimp, clams, lobster, crabs, and scallops—all relatively unlikely to be found showing up on high chair trays or kids' menus. We will therefore simply make the point for future reference that unlike fish allergies, people allergic to certain groups of shellfish (such as mollusks or crustaceans) are quite likely to be allergic to all other shellfish within the same family.

 Allergies Around the World

Apparently, certain food allergies are far more common in some places than others: Japanese have higher rates of rice allergy, Scandinavians have more codfish allergy, and a higher percentage of people in India are allergic to chickpeas than elsewhere around the world.

### Pinpointing the Problem

If you have reason to suspect that your child is having a bad reaction to something he's eating, there are several ways that you and your pediatrician can go about trying to pinpoint the problem. Unfortunately, allergies can be very complex and it may be difficult to identify a food culprit, even with special tests. Although diagnosing food allergies can be difficult, remember that the more serious your child's reaction, the sooner you'll want to seek help and come up with a plan of action.

- **Indiscriminately Eliminate.** If your first reaction is to get rid of whatever it is that "upset" your child, even before knowing just what was to blame, you can either eliminate en masse all recently eaten and/or introduced foods and gradually try adding them back one at a time, or you can eliminate the most likely suspects one at a time until the problem clears up. This approach should only be used in the case of the more mild symptoms, such as a bit of spitting up, an occasional bout of diarrhea, or an eczema flare.

- **Put Pen to Paper.** The next option is to put pen to paper and keep a food and symptom diary. Sure, the allergic effects of some foods may be immediately obvious, but others can take time and be much harder to sort out. By introducing one new food at a time, writing down what your child eats and when he eats it, and keeping track of any resulting symptoms, you're sure to pay closer attention and it may help you put 2 and 2 together.

- **Put Needle to Skin.** The 2 most common allergy tests are skin tests and blood tests. In skin prick tests, a small amount of each suspect food (or other allergenic substance) is placed on the skin and the area is punctured with a small needle. If a true allergy is potentially involved, this small exposure should be enough to trigger a rash or hives at the puncture site. Blood tests are also available that help determine if antibodies to certain foods are present. If and when food allergies present themselves, be sure to discuss the possibility of allergy testing with your pediatrician and consider requesting a referral to an allergist.

CHAPTER 32

# constipation consternation

**What do the tasks of pooping and getting one's child to eat** well have in common? They can both be quite hard at times. While this sounds like a joke our elementary school-aged children might tell and then dissolve into giggles, you will be quick to discover that a constipated child is no laughing matter. Where do food fights become involved in the discussion? At the high chair or dinner table, of course, because what your child eats (or doesn't eat) will in large part determine the shape and solidity of what's to follow. By knowing which foods are foes and which you'll want to enlist as allies, you and your child can decrease your chances of finding out about constipation the hard way.

 The Hard and Fast Rules
of Constipation

Unfortunately, not everyone agrees on the exact definition of constipation. But we can tell you that true constipation is generally defined by hard, difficult to pass, and/or infrequent poop and that many instances of childhood constipation are related to food.

### Mealtime Milestones: Food-Related Constipation Concerns

- **Newborns: The Power of Perception.** Breast milk and/or formula are generally the only dietary variables that affect how a newborn's poop takes shape. While there are certainly other causes to be aware of, parental concerns over constipation during this time may simply be a matter of perception: Not only can formula make a baby's poop take shape much more firmly than breast milk, but breastfed babies have been known to go without pooping for as long as a week or more without suffering any ill effects, despite the striking contrast with other breastfed babies who make it a point to poop after every meal.

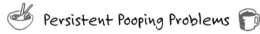

### Persistent Pooping Problems

The regular appearance of poop in the early newborn days offers the reassurance not only that babies are getting enough to eat, but also that all of the "parts" involved in making poop happen are in good working order. Conversely, when babies' intestinal tracts seem to be consistently holding something back, it may warrant further evaluation by your pediatrician, who can better assess the situation and, if necessary, test for Hirschsprung disease—a very uncommon (1 in 5,000) condition where the nerves (and, therefore, the corresponding muscles) responsible for letting it all out are unable to effectively do their job.

- **4 to 6 Months: Solid Foods Mean Solid Poops.** Once babies are fed solid foods for the first time, their poops predictably change, becoming more solid and less frequent (not to mention a bit smellier). This can be particularly distressing for the parents of previously proficient poopers or babies whose poop in the past has been anything but solid. Even in the complete absence of constipation, babies younger than 6 months are also prone to exaggeration and can create such a spectacle out of pooping—by grunting, straining, and drawing up their legs—that it may leave everyone involved a bit red in the face.

- **9 to 12 Months: Taking to Table Foods.** Some of the most popular of the table foods first given to babies include those also known for their constipation-causing capabilities. Classic examples include cheese, yogurt, bananas, and applesauce. While there is no harm in giving them, you should be on the lookout for this potentially counterproductive effect.

- **1+ Years: Difficulty Maintaining Consistency.** We are firm believers in the notion that children thrive on consistency and routine, but after 1 year of age, you may find it much harder to maintain the consistency of your child's poop for the simple reason that it will inevitably be more difficult to maintain the consistency of her diet.

---

### 🍜 Pooping by Numbers ☕

How many times children should poop in any given day is by no means set in stone, since there can be considerable variation from one child to the next, not to mention from one day to another. Formula-fed babies may only poop once every 2 to 3 days, while their breastfed counterparts may hold out for 7 days at a time without pooping *or* qualifying as constipated. That said, the number of times a child typically poops each day is as follows:

| Age | No. of Poops Per Day |
|---|---|
| 0 to 4 months | 4 |
| 4 to 12 months | 3 |
| 1 year | 2 |
| 3 years and up | 1 |

---

### *Favoring "Faulty" Foods*

We want to start by pointing out that most of the dietary causes of constipation are not inherently bad for children. In fact, they tend to be both healthy and well-loved—a combination that increases the likelihood that your child will end up eating and/or drinking large enough quantities to result in uncomfortable consequences. Start out by giving these foods to your child no more than 3 times a day, and then be prepared to cut back as needed if they prove to be too much of a good thing.

- **Milk.** Be on the lookout for one of toddlerhood's most notorious causes of constipation: too much milk. Current recommendations suggest that when 1-year-olds start drinking regular cow's milk, they no longer need the 20 to 32 ounces a day to which they (and you) may have grown accustomed. While milk may be the most predictable dietary cause of constipation, we're not convinced that it is any more constipating than its dairy counterparts, such as yogurt. Rather, milk-related constipation tends to be a matter of sheer volume.

Whether it's because they truly love their milk or they truly love their bottles and drink an exorbitant amount out of habit (see "Milk Matters" on page 65), many a child consumes far more milk than the recommended 16 ounces a day, often to the exclusion of fiber-filled foods.

- **Cheese.** Some kids find cheese especially hard to resist, regardless of whether it comes in the form of slices, strings, or shreds.

- **Other Low-Fiber Foods.** These include processed favorites such as white bread, rice, or pasta.

- **Bananas and Apples.** These are potential causes for constipation that catch the most parents by surprise. While it is generally true that eating fruit can prove to be a quick and easy cure, eating too many bananas and apples may, in fact, have the exact opposite outcome.

---

### Ironing Out Misunderstandings

When faced with a constipated infant, do not give in to the temptation to switch from "regular" to low-iron formula. While infant formulas do contain an impressive amount of iron, it's there for a very good reason: Babies need iron and the iron in formula is poorly absorbed. Even though you as an adult may have firsthand knowledge of iron's constipating abilities, don't be too quick to point fingers at iron on your baby's behalf. The amount of iron found in formula is not responsible for causing constipation.

---

### Enlist Edible Allies

As much as certain foods stand to cause constipation, so can the absence of others—typically those with a high fiber content. The good news is that by including them in your child's daily diet, you can count these foods as your friends not only in the prevention of constipation, but also its cure.

- **Bulk Up on Bran.** Fiber is not the only reason why it's a good idea to steer your child clear of sugary cereals in favor of bran-containing ones, but it certainly is a good one. Bran is best known for its high fiber content and is found in all cereal grains (including wheat, oats, rice, and corn), as well as in bran muffins, shredded wheat, whole wheat bread and pasta, oatmeal, brown rice, and graham crackers—none of which are too hard to sell to young children.

- **Pass the Ps Please.** Some of the foods best known to soften up difficult situations not only share in common a high fiber content but also the fact that they start with the letter P. These include pears, peaches, prunes, peas, and plums. B foods don't fall far behind, since beans, broccoli, and brussels sprouts are all rich in fiber as well.

- **Fruit and Fruit Juices.** For children of all ages (and even adults) fruit is perhaps the easiest and most readily accepted remedy for hard poop. Fruits that are raw and unpeeled are especially effective, once your child is old enough to eat them. When it comes to easing the pain of constipation, offering your child pure fruit juices can have the same beneficial effects as doling out the fruit. While prune juice is best known for this purpose, you may be hard-pressed to convince your child to drink it. If this is the case, we're quite partial to pear

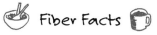

## Fiber Facts

The American Heart Association recommends getting 14 grams of fiber for every 1,000 calories consumed daily. For children ages 1 to 3 years, this works out to about 19 grams per day; for those ages 4 to 8 years, it's 25. If you're having trouble reaching these goals, aim for a minimum of your child's age plus 5 for the grams of fiber (for a 5–year-old, it would be at least 10 grams daily).

According to the US Food and Drug Administration, "high-fiber" foods contain 5 grams of fiber or more and "good sources of fiber" have 2.5 to 5 grams and may officially be labeled as such.

- **High-fiber foods:** 1 baked potato with skin; ½ cup of cooked lentils, kidney beans, black beans, or split peas; 1 cup whole wheat pasta; 1/3 cup 100% bran cereal

- **Good sources of fiber:** 1 apple or pear with skin; 1 orange; 3 or 4 prunes; 1 cup strawberries or blueberries; ½ cup wheat or bran cereal; 2 slices whole wheat bread juice—both because kids like it and because we've seen a few ounces work wonders. Apple and white grape juices may also do the trick. Orange juice, on the other hand, is not thought to be nearly as helpful as other juices or as eating the oranges themselves!

- **Water.** As simple as it sounds, water and foods with a high water content (again, fruits and vegetables) can play a major role in keeping things flowing in the right direction.

### When Food Falters: Calling in the Reserves

If you find yourself faced with a standoff and aggressive dietary measures don't soften up the situation, it might be time to call in the reserves. Be sure to enlist the help of your child's doctor when considering the use of any over-the-counter or prescription-only constipation remedy for your child—some of which may stand to give your attempts to defuse the situation a real push. Once the path has been cleared, remember that your ongoing dietary efforts will go a long way toward keeping constipation at bay.

### When the Going Gets Tough…

…the constipated stop eating. This is the final twist to the constipation story. Not only can food play a major role in causing (or curing) constipation, constipation can, in turn, set off a food fight of its own. Although there are *plenty* of reasons why children won't eat (as evidenced by many of the chapters in this book), it's worth emphasizing that constipation can definitely be high on the list. Whenever kids stop eating and/or complain of stomachaches or stomach pains, you will not only want to flip to "Food, Food Everywhere, but Not a Bite They'll Eat" on page 87, but also remember to inquire as to when they last pooped and how hard it was. After all, the number one cause of belly pain in children is…you guessed it, constipation.

CHAPTER 33

# the price of gas

**The only reason gas managed to** make its way into the pages of this book is because time and time again it has proven itself to be one of the earliest sources of mealtime stress. Why? Because when parents are faced with a gassy baby, it's only natural they want to do something about it, and as they look to lay blame where blame is due, fingers invariably get pointed at food.

While we are in no way saying that eating certain foods isn't to blame for causing gas, we've all too often seen parents go to such extraordinary and unnecessary lengths to get to the bottom of this perceived problem that it takes a lot of both foods and fun out of the eating experience. With so much time and energy (and sometimes even money) spent by concerned parents, we wanted to do our best to clear the air a bit by giving you a better perspective on what causes gas and what, if anything, you need to do about it.

### Natural Gas

To begin with, it's worth pointing out that passing gas is as expected from babies as it is children and adults. Everybody does it—14 times and anywhere from 1 to 4 pints a day, according to estimates from the National Institutes of Health. This normal bodily function unavoidably happens when air finds its way into (and out of) the intestinal tract. More often than not, this results while foods (in either solid or liquid form) are in the process of being broken down and digested.

### Do Babies Pay a Higher Price?

Given that gas is only natural, the question that arises is why do we as parents tend to overinflate the significance of gas when our babies get it? The answer is usually quite apparent: Babies often raise a much bigger stink about their gas than the rest of us. Instead of keeping their gas to themselves, they strain, cry, squirm, fuss, and fidget. In essence, we get to hear all about it. That said, we're not convinced that this display always represents an outward cry for help. In fact, more often than not it's nothing more than a nuisance. Sure, we believe gas can occasionally be quite uncomfortable. But we have a hard time convincing ourselves that your everyday, run-of-the-mill baby gas qualifies as painful. Remember—babies definitely cry for far more reasons than adults do and it's not always out of pain.

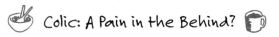

### Colic: A Pain in the Behind?

Colic is not as easily defined, or prevented, as any of us would like. It is typically characterized by excessive and unexplained crying that starts in babies by 2 weeks, reaches a peak by 4 to 6 weeks, and understandably leaves parents frantic for answers until it disappears by 3 to 4 months. While these colicky spells have long been attributed to gas and belly pain, pediatrician Dr Harvey Karp does a convincingly good job of dispelling this age-old notion in his DVD and book *The Happiest Baby on the Block*. First, the timing between gas and colic is off—since babies are born with plenty of gas, but not colic, at birth. Additionally, colic is commonly known to get much worse in the evening time, while gas problems, on the other hand, can and do present themselves 24 hours a day. In fact, as Dr Karp points out, there are cultures in which babies never get colic at all. The same does not hold true for the absence of gas.

### Why All the Hot Air?

There are 2 main food-based theories as to why babies stand to get more than their fair share of gas.

- **Taking It All In.** For some babies, excess gas is a simple matter of swallowing a lot of excess air along with all of the extra gulping, guzzling, crying, bottle use, and sucking so common in the early stages of eating and infancy.

- **Gas by Association.** Breastfeeding moms are not the only ones who may feel the effects of eating gas-causing foods, since a food's gas-causing tendencies are believed by many to be passed along in breast milk.

### Breaking Up Gas

We are big believers that there's really no need for parents to pay a high price in exchange for less gas. That said, if you find yourself going head to head with your baby's gas, there are several things you can reasonably do to try and remedy the situation—only some of which have anything

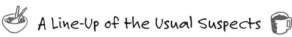 A Line-Up of the Usual Suspects

From garlic to onions to coffee and chocolate, it seems like an impressively large number of foods have been implicated as gas producers in the diets of breastfeeding moms. When it comes to singling out the culprits, start by considering the prime suspects.

- **Factor in the Fiber.** Many of the greatest gas producers are high in fiber. Rich sources of fiber include anything with bran, such as bran muffins and raisin bran.
- **Tooty Fruity.** Just about all fruits have the ability to make you toot.
- **A Variety of Vegetables.** Broccoli, onions, garlic, and cabbage most often take the heat, but brussels sprouts, artichokes, and asparagus can all have the same effect.
- **Select Starches.** Most starches are thought to cause gas, including potatoes, corn, noodles, and wheat. In fact, rice seems to be the only starch *not* found to be at fault.
- **Dairy Does It.** Milk and milk products such as cheese, yogurt, and ice cream can also cause gas, especially in those who are lactose intolerant.
- **Gas Guzzlers.** Another reason to avoid soda pop and other bubbly beverages is the carbonation they contain and the gas that is in turn transferred on guzzling.
- **A Not-So-Sweet Substitute.** Sorbitol, a sweetener commonly found in sugar-free products, is prone to causing gas (and sometimes diarrhea as well).

to do with eating. We simply suggest that you do so with only modest expectations, since breaking up gas is definitely hard to do.

- **Find Foods at Fault.** Although there are definitely some foods that are more suspect than others, identifying which ones they are in a breastfeeding mother's diet is often easier said than done. While it is certainly worth paying attention to whether or not a certain food or drink clearly causes your baby distress, just remember that food is not the only cause for gas. Be sure not to randomly remove so many foods that you leave yourself with very little on your plate.

- **Formula for Success.** Especially in a baby's early formula-drinking days, either consider holding off on mixing up powdered formula for the time being and use concentrated or ready-to-feed formula instead, or let your freshly mixed powdered formula settle before serving. The more mixing and shaking involved, the more air bubbles get into the mix—resulting in more swallowed air and potentially more gas. Be sure to discuss any formula changes with your pediatrician. When an abundance of gas is involved, trying a different formula may well be just what your doctor orders.

- **Slow the Flow.** Help your baby swallow less air by slowing the flow of liquids from his bottle into his mouth. Trial and error with different bottles and nipples tends to be the best approach.

- **Keep Things on the Up and Up.** Try stepping up your burping efforts by burping during, as well as after, each feeding. Just be forewarned—some babies don't take at all kindly to this sort of rude interruption.

- **Pump Your Own Gas.** You can help get rid of unwanted gas by simply laying your baby flat on his back and moving his legs in a bicycling motion. Better yet—give him some tummy time. This not only can help keep his head from becoming flat while strengthening his upper body, but can put a lot of pressure on any gas that's thinking about settling in to be on its way out instead.

- **Burst Their Bubbles.** While there currently seems to be no inherent harm in reaching for a bottle of gas drops to break up your baby's gas, the best tip we have for you is that we've been told you can get your money back from either the manufacturer or the pharmacy if you find they don't work! Simethicone gas drops (such as Mylicon, Little Tummys, and Phazyme) are thought to be safe to give—as often as 12 times a day, if necessary—and many parents do just that. But at approximately $12 per (30 mL) bottle, they're not exactly cheap. And studies suggest that they're not that effective either.

### The Bottom Line

If your baby has the rare type of gas that truly causes severe or persistent belly pain, or if you are concerned that her symptoms are out of the ordinary realm of infant gas, enlist the help of your pediatrician. For most babies, however, excess gas should simply be considered a fact of life. At least, if nothing else, you can rest assured that it too shall pass!

CHAPTER 34

# refluxively speaking

One of the earliest thought- and stain-provoking fights parents have with food comes up during the first several weeks and months of parenthood. After already dedicating a good deal of effort to milk delivery, whether by breast or by bottle, many of you will find yourselves wondering just how you're supposed to keep the milk you worked so hard to get in from coming right back up (and often out). Spitting up is a common occurrence that can prove to be a challenge of varying degrees of practical and medical significance. While we'll need to leave the task of figuring out how seriously to take your baby's spit-up to you and your pediatrician, we can certainly help you get a better feel for spitting up and what you can do about it.

 Reflux by Definition

You will find that several terms are used interchangeably to describe the process of spitting up including *regurgitation, gastroesophageal reflux (GER), gastroesophageal reflux disease (GERD)* or—for simplicity's sake—just plain *reflux.* According to Webster, *reflux* is defined as backward flow. In the case of spitting up, what people are really referring to is more precisely the backward flow of stomach (gastric) contents into the esophagus—hence the addition of the term *gastroesophageal.* While the terms *reflux, spitting up,* and *GER* are most often used for the normal tendencies of spitty babies, the term *GERD* or *gastroesophageal reflux disease* is typically reserved for abnormal and more severe instances when the spitting or vomiting becomes frequent or significant enough to cause pain and/or weight loss and requires more intervention.

### The Reflux "Reflex"

If you are the proud parent of a spitty baby, then you have a little muscle at the bottom of your baby's swallowing tube, or esophagus, to thank (or blame) for your spit-up challenges. This muscle—called the lower esophageal sphincter, or LES for short—sits at the top of the stomach and is in charge of making sure that whatever you give your baby to drink doesn't backslide (reflux). Instead, it helps keep food or drink moving in the right direction: from the esophagus into the stomach, and then down and out. Food fights can and do arise, however, when this muscle isn't quite strong enough, or the demands forced on it are too great to prevent an uprising. The good news: For most babies, this muscle predictably gets stronger day by day, or at least from one month to the next, and becomes more effective at keeping whatever makes its way into your baby's stomach from escaping.

### Mealtime Milestones: Keeping Milk in Its Place

- **0 to 4 Months: A Setup for Spit-up.** Faced with the formidable task of keeping milk in its place, newborns are a setup for spit-up for several reasons: They get all of their nutrition in liquid form, spend almost all of their time lying down, and often have a weaker muscle at the top of their small stomachs. While these conditions certainly improve over the course of the first several months, they may not resolve completely quite yet. In fact, one study found that more than 40% of healthy babies were still spitting up at most or all feedings at the ripe old age of 3 to 4 months.

- **4 to 6 Months: Rolling With the Lunches.** Overall, babies tend to spit up noticeably less at this age. That said, babies also begin to roll, first from front to back (around 4 months) and then back to front (by 6 months). Along with these much-anticipated rolling milestones comes an increase in the amount of outside pressure your baby's belly is sure to experience. On the flip side, your baby is also likely to start solid foods around this time, and cereal has a way of weighing things down a bit and keeping milk in its place.

- **6 to 8 Months: Sitting Sets In.** At this age, you can celebrate the fact that your baby will no longer need to take spitting up lying down. Somewhere between 6 and 8 months he will get the hang of sitting upright and as a result of this accomplishment (along with the help of gravity), the frequency of spitting up is likely to go down, if it hasn't disappeared already.

- **9 to 12 Months: On the Up and Up.** Despite the fact that some babies skip crawling altogether, this is the age when most start to crawl, scoot, or slither and soon thereafter turn themselves into true toddlers—going from hands and knees to up on their feet and on the go. While spitting up is for the most part likely to be a not-so-fond memory, don't be taken by surprise if this sudden increase in your child's mobility and the additional pressure that these new antics stand to put on his stomach get other things moving as well. At this age reflux sometimes temporarily reappears.

- **12 to 14 Months: What Goes Down Stays Down.** For purposes of spit-up prevention, table foods are going to work in your favor, and gravity stands to be a useful force in keeping things where they belong now that your toddler is spending more time standing on his own two feet. While we feel obliged to acknowledge that reflux is not a condition limited to infancy, you can take comfort and hopefully tuck away your spit rags knowing that for all but a few children, spitting up fortunately becomes a thing of the past by this age.

 **You Would Spit Up Too!**

If you calculate the amount of breast milk or formula the average thriving baby takes in over 24 hours, it adds up to about 2½ ounces per pound of weight. A 10-pound baby taking in 25 ounces per day would therefore be the childhood equivalent of a 150-pound adult drinking 375 ounces each day—that's almost 3 gallons!

## Sorting Out Your Spitter

When your baby spits up, you may feel that all is lost…or at least most of whatever it is you just finished feeding her. Admittedly, some babies are quite skilled at spitting up every last drop, but equally as likely is that the volume of what lies before you is not nearly as significant as it appears. There are several ways for you to sort out what type of spitter you have and what, if anything, you need to do about it.

- **Happy Spitters Versus Scrawny Screamers.** The term *happy spitter* has been given to babies who eat and spit up—often doing both with gusto—yet in the end do not seem bothered by their episodes of spitting. They typically make both their parents and their pediatricians happy as well by eating, sleeping, and growing according to plan without any real signs of distress. In contrast, babies with reflux who cry and seem to experience pain, don't eat well, or lose enough of what they take in to interfere with healthy weight gain better fit

### Spitters With a Cause

It's important to be aware that there can be instances in which there is more than a weak muscle at the top of a baby's stomach to blame for spit-up challenges. For approximately 3 out of every 1,000 babies, the muscle called the *pylorus* at the bottom of the stomach (whose job is to let stomach contents pass on through) gradually gets thicker and stronger, and less and less is able to get by. This condition, known as *pyloric stenosis,* typically starts out as the spit-up equivalent of a walk in the park but progresses over the course of 3 to 6 weeks into a potentially serious problem.

Spitting up becomes more frequent, involves a larger volume, and is delivered more forcefully—often referred to as *projectile vomiting* because of its propensity to come out like a rocket. Unlike happy spitters, babies with pyloric stenosis are usually anything but. If you begin to suspect your baby might have pyloric stenosis, be sure to contact your doctor immediately. The light at the end of the tunnel: An ultrasound scan of the belly can provide reassurance when it's normal, or confirm the diagnosis of pyloric stenosis and indicate the need for a straightforward surgical operation that allows food to make its way through the stomach without meeting undue resistance.

the description of *scrawny screamers* and, as such, definitely warrant both medical evaluation and, quite often, treatment.

- **Weighing In.** How much weight a baby is successfully able to gain in spite of spitting up is nothing to be taken lightly. One of the truest tests of spit-up severity is your baby's weight gain. In the grand scheme of things, it's not how much is spit back out that really matters, but what happens when it's time to weigh in. When you put all consideration of inconvenience aside, how much your baby can truly afford to spit up is going to rest in large part on what the scale and your baby's growth curves tell you.

- **Assessing Your Losses.** Overestimating one's losses seems to be human nature—especially in this instance, where you happen to find yourself wearing them. That said, you might be surprised to find that a relatively small amount of liquid can quickly turn itself into a much larger stain. If you're still skeptical and need to see it to believe it, try pouring different amounts of milk—a tablespoon versus 4 ounces, for example—onto a dry towel and see what size spot each one leaves. The point is, when your baby spits up, the situation is almost surely going to look worse than it really is. Still convinced that there's no way anything could possibly remain in your baby's stomach after she spits up? It's not necessarily time to worry as of yet, but it is as good a time as any to confer with your pediatrician.

---

### 🥣 The Changing Shape of Spit-Up ☕

Should you ever find yourself faced with sour, curdled-looking spit-up that bears an uncanny resemblance to milk gone bad, do not panic. Although it can often be disconcerting to those parents caught unaware, it is, in fact, quite normal for stomach acid to curdle things a bit. Milk that comes up in other-than-liquid form, regardless of what shape it takes or how smelly it is, generally has no more significance in the context of spitting up than its free-flowing counterpart.

## Putting a Stop to Spitting Up

While we wish we had a "quick fix" for babies who spit up, the truth
is that for a good many spitty babies, it is mostly a matter of time. But
regardless of whether or not your baby's reflux warrants watchful waiting or medical intervention, we do have some simple feeding suggestions that can help you deal with the situation at hand.

- **Avoid Topping Off the Tank.** A good way of looking at spit-up is to
  consider your baby's stomach as a gas tank that needs filling. Fill it
  too full (or too fast) and it's going to spurt right back out at you. To
  help reduce the likelihood of overfeeding, success may simply lie in
  feeding your baby smaller amounts more frequently.

- **Get Rid of Excess Gas.** If your baby is prone to spitting up, you may
  find that the extra gas in his stomach has a way of stirring up trouble.
  That's because as gas bubbles escape, they have an annoying tendency
  to bring the rest of the stomach's contents up with them. To minimize
  the chances of this happening, you can try burping your baby more
  frequently not only after, but also during meals.

- **Take the Pressure Off.** Pressing on a baby's belly right after eating can up the odds that anything in his stomach will be forced into
  action. While tummy time is important for babies, postponing it for a
  while after meals can serve as an easy and effective avoidance technique, as can keeping your baby upright for 20 or 30 minutes after
  he eats. As for positioning your spitty baby in a swing or infant seat,
  the debate continues as to whether sitting upright allows gravity to
  work in your favor or if it actually puts added pressure on your baby's
  stomach. We suggest you try it both ways and see what works.

- **Focus on the Formula.** If your baby is formula feeding, there's a
  possibility that his formula could be contributing to his spitting up.
  While some babies simply seem to fare better with one formula over
  another without having a true allergy or intolerance, an estimated 5%

of babies are genuinely unable to handle the proteins found in milk or soy formula (a condition called *milk-soy protein intolerance,* or *MSPI*—see also "Allergies and Intolerances" on page 197). In either case, spitting up may serve as one of several cues your baby may give you (along with gassiness, poor feeding, irritability, and changes in the poop) that it's time to discuss alternative formulas with your pediatrician. If your baby does have a true intolerance, a 1- or 2-week trial of hypoallergenic (elemental) formula designed to be better tolerated might be in store.

- **Have a Little Cereal With Your Milk.** Giving babies cereal before the age of 4 to 6 months is generally not recommended—with one possible exception. No, the exception is not so that your baby will sleep longer (see "Baby Bites: Starting Solid Foods" on page 21); it is to help reduce reflux. While not a fail-safe solution to the problem, giving formula thickened with infant rice cereal may help decrease how much babies with reflux spit up. If your pediatrician gives you the OK to do so, you can try this simple remedy by either adding approximately 1 tablespoon of infant rice cereal in 2 to 4 ounces of formula or looking for specially made formula with "AR" in the name (indicating that the formula already contains "*a*dded *r*ice" and is designed to be an "*a*nti-*r*eflux" measure).

### Getting Help in Fighting an Uphill Battle

If you've tried all the basic feeding tips to no avail, be sure to talk with your pediatrician about your options. Laboratory tests and studies of the digestive tract can help determine how severe the reflux is and what, if anything, needs to be done about it. Based on what you describe, as well as what the tests reveal, your pediatrician may recommend medicine(s) that prevents reflux, suppresses the acid produced in your baby's stomach, and/or treats symptoms caused by the reflux.

CHAPTER 35

# all choking aside

**We're not exactly sure what it is** about popping lollipops or hard candies into children's mouths that signals them to start running, nor do we know why they always seem to bite off more than they can chew. What we do know is that the potential to choke on food is a scary reality of childhood, and it's up to us as parents to do whatever we can to keep our children's airways clear. Food is one of the most common choking dangers for young children and poses the biggest threat for those younger than 4 or 5 years.

By making sure you are aware of the key factors that put children at greater risk and then arming yourself with the knowledge of what you can do about it, we hope to help you put all choking aside and make your mealtimes that much safer.

 A Battle of the Airways

Anatomically speaking, the trachea is the tube responsible for getting air from the back of the throat to the lungs. The esophagus is the tube that sits immediately behind it and is responsible for transporting food and drink from the back of the throat to the stomach. The little flap that guards entry to both tubes (called the *epiglottis*) acts as gatekeeper and ushers solids, liquids, and air down their appropriate paths. True choking occurs when food goes astray: Instead of heading due south into the esophagus as intended, food manages to make its way into—and proceeds to block—the airway.

## Mealtime Milestones: Developing Defense Mechanisms

- **Gag Orders.** As one of the many reflexes babies are born with, it is the gag reflex's ultimate job to serve and protect the airway. While you may initially find the sudden sputtering that it occasionally causes (when your baby is happily sucking away at breast or bottle, for example) to be quite disconcerting, you can mop up the mess and breathe a sigh of relief knowing that her protective instincts are in good working order.

- **It's a Matter of Thrust.** In addition to a fine-tuned gag reflex, babies up until the age of 4 to 6 months also have a prominent tongue-thrust or "extrusion" reflex that helps keep solid foods out of places where they don't belong. Should you be tempted to spoon in some cereal before your baby is ready to handle her solids responsibly, be prepared for her tongue to send it right back at you (see Right Back at Ya! on page 23)!

- **Sinking One's Teeth Into the Matter.** While the first baby teeth typically poke through around 6 to 8 months, it's not until 10 to 16 months that the first molars appear on the scene. Even then, it will be some time before they can be counted on for any sort of meaningful grinding and chewing of food. Until then, your child's gums and teeth can be expected to mash on small and soft solids, but that's about it.

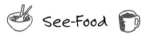

### See-Food

As children develop a sense of humor, you might find your preschooler or even younger child taking delight in showing you what's in his mouth or going so far as to pretend to gag just to get your goat. Once you ascertain that your child is not actually choking, pay no mind to his idea of a see-food diet, and this running gag is sure to quickly run out of steam.

- **Common Sense.** By the time children reach 3 or 4 years of age, they come equipped with a full set of teeth including their back molars—the presence of which, in theory, should make them better at chewing and safe swallowing. Even though what we feed kids at this age typically consists of the same foods as older children and adults, their most important defense against choking is still nowhere near fully developed. What is lacking? Good old-fashioned common sense. Until kids develop the ability to eat without distraction and outgrow the urge to play such food-related "favorites" as let's-see-who-can-fit-more-in-their-mouth and whoever-eats-faster-gets-more, you will need to keep your guard up.

### Your Best Defense: A Strong Offense

The best way to prevent your child from gagging and/or choking is to take matters into your own hands by making yourself more aware of which foods and habits are most likely to cause trouble and then commit yourself to running interference.

- **Provide Direct Supervision.** Well after your child is able to hold her own (see "Baby Bites: Starting Solid Foods" on page 21) and no longer relies on you to spoon-feed her, you'll still want to keep a close eye while she is eating to ensure her safety.

- **Size Up Your Enemies.** Kids' eyes are not only bigger than their stomachs, but also bigger than their airways. Certain foods are destined to top the list of choking hazards simply because they are the perfect size to plug up a child's airway. The most notorious include whole grapes, hot dogs, sliced carrots, and hard candy. Other foods that are small, hard, and/or tough to chew or handle include apples, nuts, and tough pieces of meat. Whenever possible, we suggest you use extra caution when serving any foods small enough to fit through the opening of

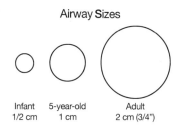

Airway Sizes

Infant
1/2 cm

5-year-old
1 cm

Adult
2 cm (3/4")

a toilet-paper roll—offering these foods with both caution and close supervision. Make sure to cut up all suspiciously sized foods before serving. Grapes should be cut at least in half, and hot dogs should be sliced lengthwise before being chopped into smaller pieces.

- **Soften Up the Situation.** Steaming, boiling, pureeing, and mashing have the ability to convert some of the more hard-to-swallow foods (such as carrots, cauliflower, broccoli, pasta, and even rice) into much more manageable mealtime fare.

- **Take It One Bite at a Time.** Some kids are so eager or in such a hurry to eat that they bite off more than they can chew—stuffing their mouths so full they resemble chipmunks storing up for the winter. Even when the individual bites themselves are likely to go down smoothly, having a mouth overflowing with just about *any* food poses an increased risk. Try offering only a few pieces at a time if you find that your child has a hard time pacing herself.

- **Avoid Sticky Situations.** Marshmallows, gummi bears, fruit roll-ups, chunks of cheese, chewing gum, and spoonfuls of peanut butter all share in common the potential to stick to the roof of the mouth or back of the throat and trip up novice eaters, potentially leading to a blocked airway.

- **Don't Stick It to 'Em.** Be extra careful and insist that your child remain seated whenever you feed her anything that comes on a stick, since a poorly timed fall could do some serious damage.

 Meals on Wheels?

However tempting it may be, allowing children to eat in moving vehicles—even if they are securely seated and strapped in—is not a good idea since it can be difficult if not impossible for the driver or another adult to attend quickly (and safely) to a child who may be spilling, throwing, gagging, or choking.

### 🍜 Talking With Your Mouth Full ☕

Although just about every parent has uttered the command not to talk with one's mouth full at least once (if not 100 times), there is an important exception to this rule of eating etiquette: If a child (or adult) appears to be choking but is still able to talk, it is actually a *good* sign, since it lends reassurance that the airway is not completely blocked.

While the well-recognized distress signal for someone who is choking is grabbing at one's throat with one's hand, it is important to realize that young children are not likely to be familiar with it. That makes the recognition of the other most concerning signs of trouble all the more important. In addition to the inability to talk, they include:

- Difficult breathing
- Noisy breathing, wheezing, or a whistling sound when breathing in
- A weak cough
- Turning blue
- Loss of consciousness

- **Eat in Place.** We'd all be at lower risk for choking by simply eating while sitting still. That said, children are especially prone to eating while doing just about anything else—dancing, singing, laughing, playing, crawling, walking, or running, to name but a few. Make sure you set aside a place for eating and insist that eating occurs in its place.

- **Don't Waffle on Safety.** Treat hazardous foods with a healthy dose of respect. No amount of whining, pleading, or begging should cause your determination to waver. If it's a matter of safety, don't give in (see "Whining and Dining" on page 95).

#### Be at the Ready

As much as all parents should hope for the best, it's important to prepare for the worst. Even if you take every necessary precaution, it is unrealistic to think that you will be able to remove all choking hazards from your child's plate (or his toy box, for that matter). It is also well established that being able to respond to a choking episode quickly and effectively is crucial in ensuring a good outcome. It is for these reasons that we second the American Academy of Pediatrics recommendation that all parents and caregivers participate in a basic lifesaving course (generally available through the American Heart Association) or an infant/child CPR course (such as that offered by the American Red Cross). What you learn could save a life!

PART VII

# in closing

**In keeping with our philosophy** of being humbly realistic about parenthood, we feel compelled to wrap up this book with a full disclosure. During the time that we were consumed with its creation, Jennifer's 5-year-old spent many a meal happily dining on chicken nuggets and hot dogs (albeit the all-natural, organic, preservative-free kind chopped up into safe-to-swallow pieces) while Laura's husband both graciously and out of necessity assumed just about all of the responsibilities involved in feeding a family of 5—from shopping to sautéing to making dinner reservations.

Bottom line—it's really not easy, nor is it realistic, to always try to have your cake and eat it too. We're not perfect parents, nor should you expect yourself to be. Quite frankly, we're convinced there's no such thing—whether you're talking about nutritional knowledge or culinary accomplishments. While we've pulled together for you a list of some of the most common food fights, and we certainly hope you use them for your own edification, please don't bite off more than you can chew.

Pick your battles wisely, pace yourself, and remember it is OK to cut a few corners of your own if and when you need to. Because in a manner very reminiscent of the creation of this book, your food fight battles are not going to come to an end overnight. Instilling children with healthy eating habits takes time, patience, perseverance, and quite a bit of trial and error. But when all is said and done, we're sure that you, too, will be justifiably proud of the fruits of your labor.

# A Close Look at MyPyramid *For Kids*

*MyPyramid for Kids* reminds you to be physically active every day, or most days, and to make healthy food choices. Every part of the new symbol has a message for you. Can you figure it out?

### Be Physically Active Every Day
The person climbing the stairs reminds you to do something active every day, like running, walking the dog, playing, swimming, biking, or climbing lots of stairs.

### Eat More From Some Food Groups Than Others
Did you notice that some of the color stripes are wider than others? The different sizes remind you to choose more foods from the food groups with the widest stripes.

### Choose Healthier Foods From Each Group
Why are the colored stripes wider at the bottom of the pyramid? Every food group has foods that you should eat more often than others; these foods are at the bottom of the pyramid.

### Every Color Every Day
The colors orange, green, red, yellow, blue, and purple represent the five different food groups plus oils. Remember to eat foods from all food groups every day.

Grains | Vegetables | Fruits | Oils | Milk | Meat & Beans

### Make Choices That Are Right for You
*MyPyramid.gov* is a Web site that will give everyone in the family personal ideas on how to eat better and exercise more.

### Take One Step at a Time
You do not need to change overnight what you eat and how you exercise. Just start with one new, good thing, and add a new one every day.

MyPyramid.gov
STEPS TO A HEALTHIER YOU

U.S. Department of Agriculture
Food and Nutrition Service
September 2005
FNS-388

USDA

USDA is an equal opportunity provider and employer

TEAM
teamnutrition.usda.gov

Source: US Department of Agriculture, 2005

# index